CAMBRIDGE LIBRARY COLLECTION

Books of enduring scholarly value

Egyptology

The large-scale scientific investigation of Egyptian antiquities by Western scholars began as an unintended consequence of Napoleon's invasion of Egypt during which, in 1799, the Rosetta Stone was discovered. The military expedition was accompanied by French scholars, whose reports prompted a wave of enthusiasm that swept across Europe and North America resulting in the Egyptian Revival style in art and architecture. Increasing numbers of tourists visited Egypt, eager to see the marvels being revealed by archaeological excavation. Writers and booksellers responded to this growing interest with publications ranging from technical site reports to tourist guidebooks and from children's histories to theories identifying the pyramids as repositories of esoteric knowledge. This series reissues a wide selection of such books. They reveal the gradual change from the 'tomb-robbing' approach of early excavators to the highly organised and systematic approach of Flinders Petrie, the 'father of Egyptology', and include early accounts of the decipherment of the hieroglyphic script.

Tell el Amarna

A pioneering Egyptologist, Sir William Matthew Flinders Petrie (1853–1942) excavated over fifty sites and trained a generation of archaeologists. He also played a notable part in the preservation of a number of cuneiform tablets that became known collectively as the Tell el-Amarna letters. Petrie's *Syria and Egypt* (1898), containing summaries, is also reissued in this series, along with many of his other publications. The present work, first published in 1894 and richly illustrated, gives an account of the work that Petrie carried out in 1891–2. It contains detailed information about both the technical aspects of the dig and the array of artefacts found, including the tablet fragments of diplomatic correspondence from the fourteenth century BCE. The chapter on the tablets is provided by Archibald Sayce, Francis Llewellyn Griffth discusses ceramic inscriptions, and the flint tools are examined by F.C.J. Spurrell.

Tell el Amarna

W.M. Flinders Petrie

CAMBRIDGE
UNIVERSITY PRESS

CAMBRIDGE
UNIVERSITY PRESS

University Printing House, Cambridge, CB2 8BS, United Kingdom

Published in the United States of America by Cambridge University Press, New York

Cambridge University Press is part of the University of Cambridge.
It furthers the University's mission by disseminating knowledge in the pursuit of
education, learning and research at the highest international levels of excellence.

www.cambridge.org
Information on this title: www.cambridge.org/9781108068390

© in this compilation Cambridge University Press 2013

This edition first published 1894
This digitally printed version 2013

ISBN 978-1-108-06839-0 Paperback

AKMENATEN

From his death-mask.

Swan Electric Engraving C?

TELL EL AMARNA.

BY

W. M. FLINDERS PETRIE, D.C.L.

WITH CHAPTERS BY

PROF. A. H. SAYCE, D.D., F. LL. GRIFFITH, F.S.A.,
AND F. C. J. SPURRELL, F.G.S.

LONDON: METHUEN & CO.
1894.

LONDON:
PRINTED BY WILLIAM CLOWES AND SONS, Limited,
STAMFORD STREET AND CHARING CROSS.

CONTENTS.

LIST OF PLATES.

I am indebted for several negatives used in Pl. I, to my friend Mr. Frank Haes, who has kindly placed them at my service. The outline of Amenhotep IV is drawn from a photograph by Mr. Backhouse, and a squeeze by Mr. F. F. Tuckett, whom I have to thank for the use of these materials.

INTRODUCTION.

1. Tell el Amarna is one of those sites which are of the greatest value for the history of Egyptian civilisation. It had a shorter life than perhaps any other town in the land. From the remaining indications it appears to have only been occupied for a single generation; and hence everything found there is well dated. The limits are even closer than at Kahun, Gurob, or Defenneh; and hence I had a particular object in exploring the ruins of the palace and the town.

After some delay I obtained permission from M. Grébaut to work in the town, but not at the tombs. I then fetched five of my old workers from Illahun and reached Tell el Amarna on 17th Nov. 1891. A few days were occupied in building huts and looking over the ground; and on the 23rd November I began work. In three days I found the painted pavement at the palace, and in a fortnight the government began to build the house to protect it; which was paid for, however, by the English Society for the preservation of the monuments. The second pavement was next found, and by the end of January 1892 the building was finished. During the remainder of my time I was occupied in cleaning and copying the painting, and fitting in a raised gangway, so that visitors could see it all, without the risk of injuring it by walking over it. At the beginning of January I had the pleasure of being joined by Mr. Howard Carter, who undertook to excavate certain parts of the town on behalf of Lord Amherst of Hackney. In this way I secured a greater amount of research, without entailing more work on myself; his special field being the great temple, and parts of the town. We finished active excavations on the arrival of Ramadan at the end of March. Work at the pavement house, drawing there, and packing our results occupied two months; and by the beginning of June

I reached the Ghizeh Museum with 132 cases. The objects brought to England were exhibited in the autumn. The representative collection of all the objects was presented to the Ashmolean Museum at Oxford, and will be exhibited in the new museum there, forming the most complete collection of the work of Akhenaten.

The survey work on the desert was done in five or six vacant days at various times. A triangulation was made in the plain, which included all the main points of the hills around; and from these fixed points I carried back all the valleys by pacing and compass, counting steps all day, and going from twenty to twenty-six miles on different days. The accuracy that can be reached by pacing and compass was better than I could have expected; the discrepancy, on a circuit of many miles up and down valleys, being only 1 per cent. of the distance.

2. We settled to live at the village of Haj Qandil, fixing at the north-east of the houses, and building a row of mud-brick huts as we needed them. Such rooms can be built very quickly; a hut twelve feet by eight taking only a few hours. The bricks can be bought at tenpence a thousand; the boys make a huge mud pie, a line of bricks is laid on the ground, a line of mud poured over them, another line of bricks is slapped down in the mud so as to drive it up the joints; and thus a wall of headers, with an occasional course of stretchers to bind it, is soon run up. The roof is made of boards, covered with durra stalks to protect them from the sun; and the hut is ready for use, with a piece of canvas hung over the doorway. Such a place is far better than a tent to live in; and on leaving we found that every native was so afraid that we might give away the materials to some one else, that we had offers for all our bricks, boards, and straw, at nearly the new price.

3. Great changes have taken place since my last volume appeared. The regulations then settled for the protection of excavators have all been swept away

B

in a fresh political bargain. For the present, however, the question is not urgent, as the new and energetic Director M. de Morgan has shewn the greatest good-will toward scientific work. Some day new and impartial conditions will have to be made about the whole department, in which at present no Englishman can hold any appointment. The personality of the Director may however prevent the need of such changes for a time.

The present excavations have been carried out in association with the same friends as before. Mr. Haworth and Mr. Kennard have joined with me in the cost, and a part of the site was worked by Mr. Carter on behalf of Lord Amherst of Hackney. Mr. Griffith, Professor Sayce, and Mr. Spurrell, have given me great assistance in their own special lines. The delay in issuing this volume is due to some illness, and to much work in connection with the organising of the new library and collections established by the will of my cordial and constant friend Miss Amelia Edwards, at University College, London. Her loss is a great blow to the popularising of Egyptology in this country ; but her bequest may, in a different manner, lead to the progress of the subject. An almost complete library, and considerable technical collections of dated objects for study, will, we may hope, induce many to follow the subject who could not do so without such assistance.

CHAPTER I.

THE SITE.

4. The ruins of Tell el Amarna lie on the eastern bank of the Nile, at the border of Middle and Upper Egypt, about a hundred and sixty miles above Cairo. They have been known throughout this century to the explorer, and are now frequented even by the ordinary travellers who come in twos and threes off the select *dahabiyeh*, and in dragoman-led streams from the tourist steamer. The sites of the temples and palace have been often plundered by the passing collector, and everything visible and portable has long since been removed from thence ; but no systematic excavation had been attempted, and no record remained to shew from where the various pieces now in museums had been taken. A few years ago a man of the village Et Till attacked the celebrated tombs in the cliffs, and cut away everything that seemed

saleable and easily removed, in the same way that the tombs of Beni Hasan and El Bersheh were wrecked, and much has now irretrievably been lost. The present century has, therefore, done its worst for the place in every way ; and all that I could hope to secure would be the most inaccessible remains of what both the ancient Egyptian and the modern Egyptologist had plundered as completely as they could. This is very late in the day to attempt any regular examination or study of such a site ; but better late than never, was all that could be said.

The name of Tell el Amarna seems to be a European concoction. The northern village is known as Et Till—perhaps a form of Et Tell, the common name for a heap of ruins. The Beni Amran have given their name to the neighbourhood, and the village of El Amarieh may be also in the question. But no such name as Tell el Amarna is used by the natives, and I only retain it as a convention, used in the same way as we use the names Leghorn or Japan. The name of the founder, commonly known as Khuenaten, is more correctly Akhenaten, which transliteration is here followed.

5. The site of the town is a wide plain on the east bank of the Nile (see PL. XXXV), hemmed in at each end by cliffs which descend almost into the river. This plain is covered with the sand and *débris* which were deposited by the prehistoric high Nile, and it is one of the most perfect sites that is possible for a great town. There is unlimited space for building, the whole plain being about five miles long and three miles wide ; this is four times the area of Cairo, and not more than a tenth of the area was actually occupied. The ground slopes gently down to the river, and the soil is clean yellow sand.

Such was the site selected by Akhenaten for his new city, and no trace has been found of any buildings or occupation of the plain at an earlier date. The ideas of the king will be dealt with in the last chapter ; but briefly we may say that, in order to carry out new principles, this king, at about 1400 B.C., left Thebes and settled at this site, and here he produced in a few years an entirely new city, in which his new ideas found free scope. His successors soon abandoned both his principles and his practice ; and within a few decades of his death every part of his construction was eradicated or destroyed with the greatest zeal. No trace of any other occupation can be found till fifteen hundred years later, when a Roman camp and town was planted on a different part of the plain. Hence we have to deal with a very brief period, and everything Egyptian found here belongs to a single generation.

6. The geological features of the plain deserve notice. Around it are four great valleys, which discharged their torrents during the ages of rainfall (see PL. XXXIV). At the north end a widely-ramifying valley, or rather three united valleys, drained the area toward El Bersheh. In the middle of the east side a long valley runs back into the desert, and was selected by Akhenaten for his tomb. South of that a shorter valley discharges between two striking headlands of cliff; and at the south-east corner is a wide structural valley, over two miles across, quite different to the other three, which are mere gorges. This wide valley drains the desert for a long way back, its branches running up north behind the other valleys. The scenery in these gorges is wild and often grand; deep clefts in the plateau wind and twist, continually altering their direction, between vertical faces of rock, two or three hundred feet high. The beds of the torrents are heaped up with fallen masses, and the path leads sometimes up a staircase of rounded blocks.

A remarkable feature is the number of depressions in the limestone strata, which are otherwise quite horizontal. Three such are seen : one at the mouth of the triple north valley, one two miles up Akhenaten's valley, and one at the mouth of a short valley a mile east of Hawata. In each case the strata are level on either side, and suddenly curve down, sometimes with faulting, to a depth of two hundred feet or perhaps more. Such a fall can only be accounted for by the collapse of a vast cavern, worn in the limestone by the subterranean discharge of rainfall to the level of the Nile at a far lower depth than at present; and hence these point to the Nile-bed being really a deeply-faulted gorge, which is now almost filled up by deposits. These depressions must have formed lakes, and have thus determined the drainage lines of their valleys.

The desert plateau, which is about 400 feet above the Nile, is not uniform in character. In some parts it is a smooth plain, only slightly grooved by shallow valleys : elsewhere it is deeply cleft by the drainage gorges, or weathered into a confused mass of broken hills and peaks. These latter usually accompany the deposits of alabaster, and are probably the result of varying hardness and resistance to weathering. The highest points of the peaks are usually masses of crystalline carbonate of lime or Iceland spar; and particularly on the hills of the north valley are spaces of many yards across, composed entirely of translucent spar glittering from every cleavage, but not clear enough for optical use, at least on the surface.

7. The alabaster quarries were worked from the earliest times. At the south-east, ten miles from the river, is the quarry opened in the IVth dynasty by Khufu. It is an open circular pit with vertical sides, about 200 feet across and 50 feet deep ; the bottom is encumbered with heaps of waste on the south part, and around the sides are crystalline faces of alabaster. It is reached by a broad sloping way cut in the rock, on the west side of which, near the pit, are the names of Khufu (PL. XLII). Elsewhere in the pit are names of Pepy I., Mehtiemsaf, and Pepy II. ; the latest name is that of an official, Sebekhotep, which shews that the quarry was used until the XIIth dynasty. This quarry was reached by a road which is traceable on the plain of Tell el Amarna, and must have started from a landing-place a little to the south of El Amarieh. It runs to the low hills, which bear a way-mark of a cairn of black stone ; this is piled up from the stones which strew the desert, the lumps of hard limestone and the flints being covered with a black-brown coating by exposure. Such cairns are thrown up on many points of the desert to direct the workmen. Passing this way-mark the road is skilfully carried past the top of a valley, and avoids all steep ground until it reaches the main range. This it ascends by the easiest way that there is in all the cliffs, and it then skirts the head of a deep valley, where it is carried by a high causeway that is still sound and firm ; this causeway has been widened and repaired in early times, perhaps by the kings of the VIth dynasty. Thence the road avoids all rough ground, and skirts the south edge of a great flat plateau, which does not drain in any direction. Groups of hut circles are found along it at different places ; and passing another valley head by a slight causeway (at C), it runs direct to the quarry. As this lies on a slope to the south, the great waste heaps around it are not seen from a distance. This quarry was first visited by Mr. Newberry, guided there by the Arabs last year ; and the inscriptions in it prove it to be the celebrated quarry of Hatnub, from whence Una obtained the alabaster altar for the pyramid of Mehtiemsaf. It seems also, by the name of Khufu, to have been the source of the great blocks of alabaster in the granite temple at Gizeh. All the inscriptions have now been copied by Messrs. Blackden and Fraser.

In the XIIth dynasty this quarry seems to have

been deserted in favour of a new alabaster quarry, **R**, about a mile to the south-west of it. In a narrow side valley there lie two quarries; the western one is partly subterranean, the entrance parts being tunnelled, and the inner part being opened to the sky. There are many tablets of the XIIth dynasty here, but as most of them were only painted they have nearly disappeared. The best is one that records a keeper of the recruits, Petuameny, under Usertesen III. (PL. XLII); others name a private person Teta. Just beyond this quarry the valley has been excavated into a shallow pit, in which there are no inscriptions. These quarries were found by Mr. Fraser, guided there by the Arabs last year.

Other quarries, **T**, lie in a valley about three-quarters of a mile to the east, but they contain no inscriptions. I found them while surveying this region. The high rock marked on the plan is a striking point from all sides; upon the top are model flights of steps, only a few inches wide, cut by the ancient workmen. There are traces of an ancient road, along the broken line on the plan XXXIV, branching at the valley head from the IVth dynasty road; pieces of alabaster lie scattered along this road, occasional way-mark stones are set up, and a group of huts occurs half-way. The valleys of these quarries slope down to the south, and evidently join into a large valley which drains into the great valley southeast of the plain.

Turning next to the northern quarries, one already noticed by Wilkinson is at the head of two valleys running opposite ways, quarry **G**. This is an open pit of alabaster, of large width, but not deep. It is approached by a sloping trench from the W., and some niches for tablets occur in the sides, and traces of a tablet now illegible; from the style it looks early, not later than the XIIth dynasty.

In a spur of the hill between the valleys is a limestone quarry, **H**, facing toward the peak of white rock on the top of the cliffs; it is cut as galleries into the cliff face, and contains the cartouche of Queen Thyi (PL. XLII), in the wide cartouche band which is characteristic of the art of Tell el Amarna. This is of importance, as proving the queen's sole regency after the death of Amenhotep III., and her adoption of the peculiarities of style before Akhenaten. I found this quarry while surveying the region.

Another quarry, **L**, contains the names of Ramessu II. and Merenptah; this is only inserted approximately, as it was found by Mr. Newberry after I had left. It seems to have been the source of alabaster for the XIXth dynasty. Strange to say, no one has yet succeeded in finding the alabaster quarry of Akhenaten; great quantities of this stone were used in the palace here, but the source is yet unknown, although I followed up every road that I could find.

8. The ancient roads are of four classes: (1) the patrol roads of the *mazau* or police; (2) the roads to the quarries; (3) the roads to the tombs; (4) the roads to the steles.

The patrol roads run from end to end of the plain, or along the crests of the hills, or into the desert. They are marked out by the pebbles being swept off from ten or twenty feet width of ground, and heaped in a ridge on either side: or in more remote parts they are merely indicated by way-marks on the ridges of the country. In the plain they take advantage of any rise of the ground to run over it and command a view; the foothill in the middle of the plain was a favourite point of inspection, and every road but one runs over it. An isolated round hill at the foot of the southern range was also a look-out station. That these roads were only for patrols is proved by their nature; they run up slopes on the hills which would be impossible for a chariot, while easy ascents could be found near by; in the long desert road the straight line is carried across the tip of a spur with a rise of 20°, instead of turning round it. Such roads then could not be for royal chariot drives, nor for transport of stones, but rather like our coastguard paths to keep the patrols from wandering off the line in the dark. In the plan (PL. XXXV) the connections of the roads are unfortunately not completed, owing to my foot being disabled during the last weeks of my stay at Tell el Amarna; Mr. Carter very kindly completed the survey this year, but his map with all the notes was lost in the post. The roads were really continuous from end to end, but are much broken up and washed away in many parts by the torrents from the valleys. The roads along the crests of the hills are also for patrolling, and not for travelling. The road is very well defined where it passes above the stele **U**, and runs on without hesitation to the small valley south of the stele. Here it abruptly ends, at a sheer fall of about three hundred feet, and is resumed on the other side in the same line. No man could possibly get across, or even climb down and up, at this point; and, if transit had been required, it would have been quite easy to diverge around the head of this little valley. There is no sign of such a continuation, however, and the roads must have been used by patrols who only needed each to secure their own beats and to challenge each other across the valley when they approached at the ends of the roads. The long road running into the desert near this point is also a patrol road by its steep gradients for short distances. It is on the whole most skilfully laid out to skirt across the heads of the valleys which run either way, and keep the highest and most even ground. It is well made near the beginning, and gradually deteriorates, until it is only marked by occasional stones; and it does not lead anywhere in particular, but is untraceable beyond a wide valley, which runs south, beyond the limits of this map (PL. XXXIV) The roads to the quarries we have already noticed.

The roads to the tombs are the best known of these roads, and are entered on the map of Lepsius (Denk. I. 63); but they were only there surveyed by their bearings from the tombs, without actually tracing their course on the plain. They were probably used both for the workmen, and for the funeral processions. The northern tombs have roads converging, and leading to a square enclosure. Within this are remains of several mounds, of which an enlarged plan is given in PL. XLII. The northern mound has a brick wall enclosing a square space filled with desert sand, a large part of which I dug out fruitlessly; it was evidently a basis for some object, as four ascents lead up to it, one on each side. The middle mound has one ascent, and two small mounds by it. The southern mound has four ascents, which suddenly break off before touching the mound; it seems to have been cased with stone which has been removed, leaving these gaps on each side. From the figures of great altars with sloping ascents, shewn in the views of the temple court in a tomb here, and the altar with sloping ascent at Der el Bahri, it seems that these are a group of altars, probably intended for offerings on behalf of the occupants of the northern tombs.

9. We now pass to the steles, which are more fully shewn on this map (PL. XXXIV) than in any previous account, though probably there yet remain others to be discovered. They are here lettered with discontinuous letters, so that others may be inserted in the series in future, without upsetting the lettering here adopted. We begin with the western bank.

Stele A.—This bears the king and queen on the north side of the scene at the top, adoring the Aten southward. 8 columns of inscription and 25 lines. On the south of the stele are two pairs of statues of Akhenaten and Nefertythi holding altars before them with two daughters in relief; but with three daughters—Atenmeryt, Atenmakt, and Ankhsenpaten—incised on the sides of the altars. The stele is carved on a good face of rock, but much of it is weathered away. It is published in Prisse, Mon. Eg. PL. XIV.

Stele B.—This is two miles south of stele A, on the most striking cliff along the western desert, the prominent corner of which towers up vertically, and is known as El Qalah, or "the castle." It has figures of the king and queen and two daughters repeated on both sides of a central altar and Aten disc, in the top scene. 7 columns of inscription and 27 lines. On each side of the stele are statues of the king and queen holding altars. It has been much disfigured by Arabs in 1885, who have hammered on names, Reshwan and Said, and date (1)303. Portions of the upper inscriptions are published by Lepsius (Denk. III, 91, a–f). M. Daressy (Recueil XV, 61) writes of statues near Dirweh "mais la stèle n'a pas été gravée ou a disparu." Either there are some monuments besides stele B which escaped my examination, or else he has not visited the place, nor seen stele B.

Stele F.—This is on a low scarp of rock, in the middle of a wide bay of desert. The exposed part is entirely destroyed, but by scraping away sand with my hands I uncovered parts of 10 lines, the last 6 being complete. It does not seem to have been known to any one in modern times. The whole stele contained a scene 41 inches high to the under-edge of the Aten disc, and 14 lines of inscription, 55 inches wide. A road runs from it toward Gildeh, as the town is actually called, though the maps name it Dilgu. South of this I have searched all the cliff faces for fifteen miles, up to Mair, without finding any more steles.

10. Crossing now to the eastern bank, the southernmost stele that I have seen is stele J, and none is to be seen for about two miles south of this. This has a scene of the king, queen, and one daughter, adoring the Aten, on the south side of the altar. 8 columns and 9 lines of inscription remain; but the rock is very bad, and has been largely inlayed with pieces now lost, and the whole of the lower part is gone, leaving a great cavity. The rock is smoothed on the north of the stele, as if to begin the usual statues in recesses.

Stele K is the longest of all. It has a scene of the king and queen and one daughter adoring the Aten, and two other daughters have been added later beyond the margin. The whole was originally 79 lines long; but the 40th is the last visible, besides traces of numbers 74–79 at the bottom. This probably is the same which Lepsius gives in Denk. III, 110 b., as it seems to be indicated on his map, but misplaced.

Stele **L** is a small tablet almost entirely weathered away, only one or two signs being traceable. It is about twenty yards north of the Shekh's tomb at the corner of the hill.

Stele **M** is about ten yards north of **L**. It has the king and queen and two princesses on the south side of the scene, adoring the Aten. 8 columns and 8 lines of inscription, but the lower part quite weathered away. Spaces on each side appear to have contained statues now destroyed.

Stele **N** has the king, queen, and one daughter on the west side of the scene; the second daughter has been added later. The inscription has been largely cut on inlayed pieces which are now lost, but it accords with stele **S**. 19 lines are visible, and more is buried in the sand. On each side are flat recesses, which probably contain statues now buried. A road leads from the plain up the hill to this stele. The scene is given by Lepsius, Denk. III, 110 a.

Stele **P** is in tolerable condition, and appears to be that published by Prisse, Mon. Eg. XII.

Stele **Q** was only discovered by Mr. Newberry in 1893, since I left; hence the position is approximate.

Stele **R** shews the king, queen, and two daughters. It is much injured, partly by loss of inlayed pieces, and also by scandalous destruction in late years in the attempt to chop out pieces, in the same style in which the tombs are wrecked.

Stele **S** is by far the most complete and beautiful of all. It has figures of the king, queen, and two daughters on each side of an altar, adoring the Aten. It is 5 feet wide and 8 feet 3 inches high. A photograph and copy is published by M. Daressy in Recueil XV, 52, but I cannot agree that Prisse professed to publish this in his PL. XIII, which rather seems to me to be stele **P**, not seen by M. Daressy. The list given by this explorer only contains eight, and he has not seen **B** (?), **F, J, K, P, Q**, or **V**. A complete squeeze of it was taken by me; and a plaster cast was exhibited with the antiquities from Tell el Amarna, and is now preserved at University College, London. The condition of the stone is marvellous, no appreciable weathering or loss having taken place on it, although it is fully exposed.

Stele **U** is the largest of all, being 14¼ feet wide and about 26 feet high; it is on the side of a bay of the cliffs with a road leading up to it across the plain. The king, queen and two daughters are on the south side of the scene adoring the Aten. 3 columns and 24 lines of inscription, most of which is perfect. On either side is a recess with statues of the king and queen more than life-size, holding altars; although battered, the king's head yet remains on his northern statue. The inscription I copied by telescope from the opposite side of the bay. It is published—with many errors—by Prisse in Mon. Eg. XII.

Stele **V** is extremely weathered away; so much so, that though close to the well-known tombs, it had never been noticed until I searched for it in consequence of noticing the road running up the hill to it. There are only about a dozen signs remaining, including a mention of a tablet, the distance between the tablets, and the end of an Aten cartouche. Stone walls have been built in front of it forming several chambers (see PL. XLII); but these are probably of later date, when many habitations were formed in these cliffs, especially behind some rock masses between steles **U** and **V**, where the face of the cliff has slipped forward and left a long tunnel behind it. These dwellings appear to be of the late Roman age by the pottery thrown out; possibly due to refugees from the Roman town in the plain, at the Arab invasion.

It seems almost certain that other steles have existed on the bold cliff north of the plain. But I carefully searched the whole of the face as far as the mouth of the valley beyond the corner, and although the cliff faces are magnificent, both for surface and position, not a trace of a stele can be found. As two plain tomb facades remain there in perfect condition, nothing has disappeared from weathering. We can only say that if steles existed here, they must have adjoined the quarries over the river, and have been destroyed by later quarriers working there. The text of these steles is usually the same, but **K** contains a longer and apparently different account. The subject of the standard text records that a district named Akhutaten, with its villages and inhabitants, was dedicated to the Aten, and gives the length of the district between the terminal steles from north to south, in the sixth year of Akhutaten, who swore never to pass outside of these boundaries. In the eighth year he recorded a visit of inspection to the south-eastern tablet, and confirmed his oath.

CHAPTER II.

THE PALACE.

11. The position of the palace of Akhenaten is evident from the nature of the buildings. There are but three sites possible—the two marked "temples" and that marked "palace" on the plan (PL. XXXV), as there are no other buildings of great extent. The "great temple" site is not suited for the palace, as it only contained one main building, and that situated a long distance from the river. The other "temple" site also only contained one building, not very large, and approached through great pylons. But the site marked "palace," on the other hand, cannot be a temple, as it will be seen from PL. XXXVI that it has not a single usual feature of the temples. On the contrary, the numerous painted pavements in it, the grouping of several structures of varied form and elaborate finish, the presence of vase fragments with the king's name, with pieces of Aegean pottery, and the situation opening to the river-bank all along, point to this as being clearly the royal palace. I therefore excavated over nearly all of the site, and have recorded the varying remains which I found on PL. XXXVI.

There are four kinds of remains to be traced—(1) the brick buildings, which are marked in solid black; (2) the stonework columns and bases in the brick buildings; (3) the foundations of the stone walls marked as a double line of blocks. In all cases the stones have been removed down to the very lowest, and not a single block was found in place; but these foundations, being deep, have left a wide trench in the native sand where they were extracted, which is now filled with chips and earth; and by tracing these trenches, often 6 or 8 feet deep, we could follow the lines of the walls. (4) There are broad cement beds, marked here by diagonal shading. Whether these supported buildings or pavements we cannot be certain.

12. We will begin at the south end of the site. Here we meet the great hall of brick pillars, surrounded by a double wall, which also runs the whole length of the palace next to the high road. Probably this was arched over above, and supported chambers on the walls; but the sides are still upright for 8 or 9 feet in some parts. The object of this double wall would seem to be as a protection against thieves, as three or four men in such a passage could guard the whole palace from any one attempting to dig through the mud-brick walls. The open spaces at the south end are not understood. They are about 3 feet lower than the ground level, and therefore seemed at first sight like fish-ponds. But on clearing around the edge nothing was found but clean native sand at the bottom, and it would have been impossible for them to hold water. There is a similar enigma in the town, where I uncovered a pit about 100 feet square and 10 feet deep; it was lined with a brick wall and surrounded by a brick paving, but the bottom was only clean sand. There is no entrance to the hall here, all three walls being solid across the middle line.

The great hall is 423 ft. 4 ins. wide, and 234 ft. 7 ins. long; it contained 542 pillars, each 52 inches (2½ cubits) square, and with spaces of 107 inches (about 5 cubits) between them. The middle passage is 173 inches wide, or about 8 cubits. The pillars are all of mud-brick, but very little remains of them, the site having been all apparently dug for earth; and we learn more from the other halls to the north, which were undisturbed. In these the pillars are also 52 ins. square, but rather closer together, being from 98 to 104 ins. apart. Each hall contains 40 pillars, making 702 in all the halls. These pillars were white plastered, with a small torus-roll up the corners, and the ceiling was of mud plaster, painted with vine-leaves and bunches of grapes on a yellow ground. The purpose of these great halls seems to have been for a cool shade to wander in during the heats, the great mass of the pillars serving to cool the air, and rendering this almost like a subterranean retreat. In the southeast corner of the south-east small hall, many wine and oil-jars had been cast aside; they mostly bore dates in the year 2, which appears to be of the reign of Akhenaten's successor (see Chap. V.); hence these halls were then falling out of use and becoming lumber-holes. It was probably at this time that the doorway to the great hall was walled across, as I found it, the gates having been removed and a brick wall run across the pivot blocks. The purpose of thus cutting it off was probably to prevent thieves harbouring in its forest of pillars, when it had become disused. Not a chip of stonework was found in the whole of these halls, except the sill and pivot-blocks of the great doorway.

13. Outside the halls at the north-east is a series of store-rooms, and it was in these that the blue paste fragments of a vase, with the names of king and queen, were found (PL. XIII, 27), along with other fine pieces; and in the passage in the wall were pieces of Aegean pottery, engraved glass (PL. XIII, 36), &c. This set of store-chambers appears to have been added after

the thick wall was built, leaving only a narrow passage at the corner of that.

Beyond this the stone foundations seem to be without any regularity, and we cannot guess at the design of the building. All we can glean is that a great entrance way ran along the line marked "alabaster pavement," as several massive blocks of alabaster were found in this trench, each with figures of bound captives, like those on the passage way of the painted pavement. Also near this, on the north, were large bases and portions of capitals, and an abundance of the stone hieroglyphs from inlayed inscriptions, shewing this to have been a highly-ornamented part of the palace.

Coming more to the east, remains of two alabaster steles were found, lying on two slightly-raised bases of small blocks and cement. The gap in the cement bed between these, being all clean sand, seems as if it was an entrance, with a stele on each side. But the purpose of the cement bed is yet unexplained. These steles are all of one type, shewn in PL. XII, 2. They are found in all materials. A hard white limestone one in the great temple enclosure is inscribed on both sides (now placed in the pavement house); pieces of red quartzite, black granite, and red granite steles are found in the temple and elsewhere, and alabaster steles in the palace. It seems as if every important place were signalized by a dedicatory stele to the Aten. All the steles are alike in design; the ends are not wrought, but the top has a curved surface between the rectangular edges, with large cartouches on it, and the line of the top is always sloping slightly down to one end. The object of this peculiar form is unknown.

Returning to the south-east, we see a small cement platform which must be for an isolated building. North of it is a small brick building; north of that a mass of brickwork, with a cement bed adjoining it, at the east edge of which, and in the trench of foundations, were found the fragments of the vine columns (PL. VIII). The middle of the length of the palace is marked by a great pylon or gateway, of un-Egyptian form, across the main road; it had two footways, and a wider chariot-way, between them, like a Roman triumphal arch. The side walls run deep back into the structure of the palace, and that of the large house on the other side of the road; and the depth of these suggests that they were needed for arch abutments, and that the ways were arched across.

North of this are varied small buildings. One contains painted pavements in almost every room (marked P on the plan); and in the chambers east of this some pieces of stone column were found. The reeds of these were not grouped, but were similar all round, and treated angularly (see PL. VII, 1).

14. The only part of the palace which shews a regular plan is the building against the outer wall, on the north east (see PL. XXXVI). Though part of it is wholly washed away by denudation, we can trace a symmetrical design in the remains. From the retired position of this, in the innermost part of the palace enclosure, from the fine ornamentation of the floors covered with painting, from the elaborate stonework, the gorgeous glazed-ware decoration, the number of sleeping cubicles, and the queen's name and titles fully set out on the well-coping, it seems most likely that this was the queen's pavilion, or *harem*.

The entrance seems to have been at the southern end of the pile, as there were no considerable chambers north of the cubicles. Of the first hall, marked "Painted pavement," only the north and east sides remained, and a part of the painted floor along those sides. This led to a wide cross-chamber, 21 feet 4 inches long, and 51 feet 3 inches across, the painted floor of which is almost perfect (PL. II). Thence the door led into the open Court; and the central object in that was the well, covered with a canopy supported on finely-sculptured pillars. This well must have been the main point to the eye, in looking along the axis of the building through the open doorways. Of this Court one base of a column remained, shewing that it had a colonnade around it. The wall at the sides was probably open above to light the side passages, like the dwarf walls and pillars of Thothmes III at Medinet Habu. The passage roofs were supported by a row of stone columns down the middle, the fragments of which lead to the restoration given in PL. VII. The cubicles opening off the passage are remarkable. They are 6 × 8 feet in plan. Within the doorway is a thin wall 13 inches from the doorway, and 8 inches thick. And in the two back corners of the chambers are blocks of brickwork, 21 inches wide and 24 inches deep back. The purpose of these seems to be for supporting a sleeping bench along the back of the chamber, 2 feet wide and 6 feet long; while at the sides ran other benches, 15 inches wide and 5 feet long, on which to sit or to place personal articles. These side benches being supported on dwarf walls, clear of the door wall, left space for a curtain to hang down over the doorway to screen the room. The original height of these benches, the supports of which are mostly ruined, is shewn by the plastering above the supports, which is 33 inches from the floor. This is the first time that the arrangement of bedrooms has been traced in Egypt. The larger rooms on the south, with one central pillar, and two small rooms opening from them, might be for some chief attendants, as the size—10 × 12 feet—is not enough for a common hall. The queen's private room might be the side hall marked P 1, which was the most highly decorated part, the columns having been covered with glazed-ware modelling of plants. The courtyard was probably closed along the north side by a colonnade which is now destroyed. In the court stood the well we have noticed. This was only shallow, about 15 feet deep, and quite irregular at the bottom. The upper part was lined with stone, and pieces of a stone coping with rounded top lay near it, doubtless from the dwarf wall around it; these bore the full titles and name of the queen (base of PL. X). The fragments of the beautiful pillars found around it will be noticed further on. As this well was only filled during the inundation, water was needed from a greater depth at other times; and a *sakkieh* or water-wheel appears to have existed at the other end of the court. The remains of it are indicated by two deep trenches in the ground, about 2 feet apart, from which the natives have lately abstracted all the stone; the stone walls which were here seem to have been the sides of a pit for the water-wheel and chain of jars, to draw water from a depth.

The fragments of colossi of quartzite and red granite, shew that outside of this *harem* building must have been one of the most decorative parts of the palace. But the wide expanse of open sand, on which no trace of remains now exists, prevents any conclusions about this. It may have been an open court or parade-ground; and upon the cement basis possibly stood the high gallery facing the north, from which Akhenaten is represented throwing down wreaths to the people. Further north are remains of a building with blocks of mortar paving, concrete hearts of walls and sculptured fragments, and outside of that a long deep foundation of a wall, which seems to limit the palace in this direction. As the trenches, (which shew where the natives have dug for stone in the foundation lines), run down into the cultivated ground toward the river, and the river level must have risen here as elsewhere, it seems likely that more of the palace extended westward toward the river; and it is possible that we have only the back of it remaining here, and that the whole of a symmetrical river frontage has been lost under the crops.

Certainly the absence of any scheme in the greater part of the structures is surprising, as the whole was executed at one period. But there seem signs of a change of design, as a very long deep foundation can be traced just west of the *harem*, and running south for 600 feet without any connection with adjacent buildings : and the large isolated brick building in the middle of the area runs across a similar deep foundation. The store-rooms and painted rooms, P, also seem to have been forced into the plan with little regard to the larger works. As however not a single fragment of sculpture earlier than Akhenaten was found anywhere, and not any name later than his on the sculptures—except Horemheb once in the great temple—we must attribute any changes to the rapidly-developing ideas of Akhenaten, rather than to a succession of rulers.

15. We now turn to the architecture.

The only columns that can be restored directly are those of the gallery in front of the cubicles. The various fragments found there indicate the form shewn in PL. VII, 3. For restoring these we have the bases of the columns, pieces of the spring of the stems to the first band, an intermediate band, the large upper band, the ducks, the band above, and the lower part of the capital; the top of the capital I have reduced from a fragment of a great capital of this palace. The only point of doubt is the number of intermediate bands : I have allowed one, (which is left blank here) as being likely from the proportions. According to the columns in the rock-cut tombs the height would be but 3·4 diameters to the base of the capital; this proportion would exclude an intermediate band here, and so reduce this column to 3·5 diameters or 65·7 inches, *i.e.* 77 with the capital. As however this seems unduly low, and rock-cut columns are generally thicker than others in their proportions, I have credited this column with one extra band, thus raising it to 4·1 diameters. The lotus capital columns of Sety I and Ramessu II are 3·7 and 4·5 diameters, so that 4·1 is just the average. The portions of inscription on the bands shew exactly how much has been recovered. The type of the columns is an imitation of 8 bundles of reeds, each bundle shewing 4 reeds on its outer surface, which is thus composed of 8 segments of circles, each broken into 4 smaller segments. This reeded part was coloured a yellow olive. The springing leaves at the base and at the capital are coloured brownish pink. The corresponding parts of the glazed columns of the S.E. painted chamber are apple green, and brown, puce, or yellow. The bands

c

are painted yellow, with blue in the incised hiero-glyphs : probably these were engraved bands of bronze, on the glazed columns.

This type of column was varied slightly in the small chambers of the block south of the *harem*. Here the reeds were not grouped in bundles, but all uniformly ranged around, and each treated angularly with an edge outside, as in PL. VII, I.

Both of these types of columns were used in the palace front, as is shewn by the fragments found on the western side. But the size in this part was far larger, some columns being as much as 5 feet diameter; hence their height in proportion would be 20 feet, and the capital 3 feet more, or altogether nearly the size of the columns of the Ramesseum.

16. Some other varieties of type were also used here. The pieces of palm leaf and date capital (PL. VII, 4, 5, 6) shew a design which is not met with again until the Ptolemaic times. But the most striking of all these capitals must have been those inlayed with coloured glazes. These capitals were of the old palm leaf form (PL. VI), which was known in the XIIth dynasty, and was used down to Roman times. Instead, however, of merely indicating the ribs and leaves, they were developed by inserting alter-nating colours along the leaves, and then the inter-vening lines of stone were gilded. Thus the capital was a copy of the favourite cloison work of the Egyptian jewellers, in which minute segments of rich stones were set each in a fitting nest of gold, so as to pro-duce a brilliant device, in which every spark of colour was separated from the next by a line of gold. Such, indeed, was the main principle of the use of gold and light colours in Egypt, to serve as a brief break between larger spaces which might otherwise harshly interfere.

Here the jeweller's design was boldly carried into architecture on the largest scale, and high capitals gleamed with gold and gem-like glazes. Not to be wasteful the Egyptians often substituted mere painting for all this gold and inlaying, probably in the parts which were less open to daylight. The actual evidences that we have for this are painted pieces of such capitals with the hollows alternately red and blue, and the ribs and bars all yellow; pieces of capitals of exactly the same form with the hollows filled with coloured glazes let in; and pieces of glaze which still retain the edge of the gilding adhering round their edges, although all gilding has perished from the limestone. This edge of gilding sufficiently shews that the parts otherwise painted yellow were actually

gilded in the more costly inlayed capitals. In the restoration there is no direct evidence for the colour of the bands below the capital; but pieces of columns with wide bands of red and blue were found in the smaller temple, and on this capital the broad gold rib is flanked by blue glaze next to it; hence the restoration that I have adopted.

17. Two other types of columns are quite peculiar to this place. Those of the well in the *harem* court were surrounded by bands of figures of the king, queen, and princesses adoring, and with bands of decoration not found elsewhere. In PL. X the frag-ments of these are drawn. At the top is a chequer net-work, the traces of colouring on which shew that the net lines were yellow, and the spaces red and blue chequerways. Next is a regular Egyptian garland of lotus petals threaded together; and below that a scale pattern. These elements apparently occupied this relation, as the fragments shew us; a continua-tion is carried out in broken line to connect the design. Another design was of spiral pattern; which, though common in colouring, is not known otherwise in Egyptian sculpture. The raised spiral was yellow, and the spaces alternately red and blue. Below it came a garland; and then a zigzag pattern. The position of these bands in relation to the figures is not known. The fragments of figures and car-touches shew delicate work, but nothing fresh in design.

The other peculiar type of column was found in the region marked "vine columns." The form was as strange as the decoration, many of the fragments not belonging to circles, but shewing irregular flattened sections, as if even the cylindrical column had been abandoned, and variety and naturalism sought by copying the curves of tree trunks. The surface decoration (PL. VIII) is unique in Egypt, and can only be paralleled in mediæval art. Winding branches of a climbing vine twist around the column in wild con-fusion, their leaves turning in all directions and over-lapping, with a pointed disregard of any symmetry or pattern. The pieces found have been arranged on the plate so as to give some continuity in the stems, in order that the design may be more easily grasped; but none of them really fit, and some are of limestone, others of soft sandstone.

Much the same decoration is shewn on two pieces of the great stele of the temple (PL. VIII, top). It evidently represented the king, queen, and princesses, life-size, adoring the Aten; and over the top of the stele hung a mass of trailing vine (using the word in its wide sense, as a climber) which seems to be the convolvulus or woodbine, covering over all the blank spaces of the tablet.

Some pieces of foliage capitals are shewn in PL. IX. One is fully carved with a close mass of leaves; another is merely sketched with incised lines; but both of these are irregular in outline, and accord with the erratic forms of the columns. Some other fragments of leaf-work are shewn on the same plate. The piece of a small column has the band of uraei around it which occurs on columns in the rock tombs; with a garland of lotus flowers above it, and then developing into a bunch of papyrus stems.

18. Of the architraves and flat stonework nothing was found except a few small doorways of the cubicles. All of the rectangular stones have been removed from the town for use elsewhere; but the columns being sculptured around, could not be re-used by reversing them like the squared stones, and hence the sculptured faces were often struck off in flakes and left on the ground. The doorways of the cubicles had jambs of limestone, with the usual royal names and titles down them; the lintels were also of limestone with cavetto moulding above, and bore the cartouches of the Aten, of the king, and of the queen. These slabs of limestone were merely thick enough to face over the brick jambs and lintels, and the lintel-stone had large rough holes in projecting lugs at the sides, apparently to pin it back to the wall by wooden pins. All this limestone work was painted yellow, and the incised hieroglyphs coloured red and blue. The examples of these lintels and jambs were brought away, and are some at Ghizeh, and others at Oxford.

19. Of the decorative sculpture we have already noticed that which belongs to the different orders of the architecture on the columns. On the walls, scenes appear to have been represented, as in the tombs. A few fragments of such were still left, such as those on PL. XI, where Nos. 1, 3, 6, 7, 8, 9 are all from the palace; Nos. 2 and 4 come from a sculptor's school, No. 5 from the great temple, and Nos. 10–12 from workshops. The execution of the horses is very slight and rough, but is true to nature; indeed it is remarkable how well the artists of Akhenaten succeeded with the horse, as in the two spirited rough heads PL. I, 4 and 8. The Egyptians seldom drew the horse well, yet in these three examples, one from a wall, PL. I, 4, sketched on a pot, along with a hawk and many other subjects, and PL. I, 8, from a sculptor's trial piece, it would be difficult to improve

within the limitations of such work. The group of pigeons hung up (PL. XI, 6) is also carefully characterised by the necks and heads, different from those of the groups of ducks on the columns. The block (PL. IX) with the deer, is of sandstone, and was found in the palace near the "bases of columns."

Among the figures the old man (XI, 2) is merely a trial piece, but the student has seized well on the characteristics of age. How learners began their studies is shewn by the elementary trial piece (XI, 4) with neb signs; the first of which is well-cut by the master, the others shewing varying care in the pupil. The man sitting asleep, (XI, 7), the foreigners (XI, 8), and the servants at work making mixtures (XI, 9), are all parts of large scenes, which shew how much has been lost. A curious class of pieces apparently come from some workshop. Nos. 10, 11, 12, PL. XI, are all alike carved on slabs of limestone, which are rudely smoothed at the edges; they were not cut from any larger sculpture, nor were they ever inlaid in any wall, as the edge is rounded so that no good joint could be made. That they are not trial pieces is seen by the careless work of 10, the incomplete signs and the painting on 11, and the limbs not being finished in 12. The only explanation of these seems to be that they were blocks prepared in the town, ready to be fitted into defective places in the rock tombs, where they would be trimmed to make a close fit. As the sculpturing of the figures would occupy some time, it was done in the more convenient place in advance; and the hands and feet of the figure 12 were left unfinished in order to make up the connection with the rest of the scene.

The steles placed in the chambers of the palace have been already noticed. The upper one PL. XII is carved deeply in very fine hard limestone, and was found in the great temple. The two steles in alabaster were found in the palace.

20. Another branch of sculpturing was developed in the abundant use of inlaying. This was found only at the west side of the palace, and about the massive foundations near the entrance of the temenos of the great temple. It is but seldom that the inlaid hieroglyphs have lasted in their settings through all the shocks of the breaking up of the stones; the more so as the hollows and the pieces are usually much rounded, and the workmen trusted more to the plaster than to fitting. A favourite stone for being thus inlaid, was the extremely hard smooth white limestone. In the temple enclosure parts of a cornice of this were found, and dozens of black granite

and red quartzite pieces for inlaying. Another block there was inlaid with glazed work ; a flying duck, naturally painted, still occupying its place. In the palace some flakes of the blocks of stone were found with the hollows for the inlaying, and with some pieces still in place. These were black granite inlayed in yellow quartzite ; white alabaster in red granite ; black obsidian, red quartzite, red limestone, and black granite in white limestone. But most of the remains consisted of loose hieroglyphs, which had been lost out of the inlaying when the palace was quarried and destroyed. These pieces were mostly in black granite, and comprised borders of cartouches, *kheper, maāt, nefer, heq*, and many other signs common in the inscriptions of this reign. The enormous labour required to form the slender signs in such a brittle material as black granite is truly astonishing. But in smaller work they economised by using glass rod for the thin lines while retaining stone for the wider pieces.

21. Beside thus inlaying stone in stone, much was done by inlaying coloured glazed hieroglyphs in stone. The flying duck has just been mentioned ; and in the palace ruins many pieces of signs were found, some of unusual size. Discs of Aten, with the regular serpent pendant, are some of them six inches or more across, made in dark red ware ; borders of cartouches are three or four inches wide ; and large green reed signs, and others, all shew that great inscriptions, intended to be seen from a distance on the palace walls, were blazoned out in gorgeous coloured glazes set in the white limestone.

22. Beside the use of glazes for inlaying in sculpture, they were used to inlay patterns in the stone, apparently up the sides of the door-jambs, and in such places, much as they were used in the gilded capitals of the great columns. The columns in the south-east hall (PL. XXXVI, p. 1) of the harem, appear to have been entirely overlaid with glazes, as not a fragment of sculpture was found in that room ; but there were dozens of pieces of glazed tile, moulded to represent the bundles of reeds which are shewn on the columns in the adjacent passage of the cubicles. These tiles are fluted to imitate pairs of the reeds, and end in narrower projections, evidently to be retained by a band on the column. Probably, from the colouring on the painted stone columns, the bands were of gilded bronze, which would compare well with the rich green of the glazing. Many triangular lotus-flower pieces, with buds to fit between them, and loose petals, with intervening pieces, were also found

in the chamber, and probably belonged to the decoration around the capitals of the columns.

Glazed tiles were also used, painted with plants and flowers ; the most common were green tiles with the thistle and daisy, which appear to have extended the whole length of the west side of the great hall of columns, as pieces were found at intervals all along that wall. But they had evidently been removed as complete as possible, to decorate some other place ; and from the broken parts left all of the inlaid daisies, except one, had been picked out. The other tiles were painted with groups of papyrus, thistles, figs, &c., and were found scattered in the palace, mostly about the store-chambers nearest to the halls of columns. In the same region were the pieces of glazed table-dishes, imitating half-gourds, half-fishes, &c., which shew that the royal table-service was an anticipation of modern taste. The other details of the glazed ware will be noticed in Chap. IV on the manufactures.

23. The paintings are the most complete and striking remains found in the present excavations. All the pavements were left by me in place, and the three most perfect halls, those of the *harem*, are now protected by a building under guard. These pavements were formed by laying a floor of mud bricks on the soil, covering them with a coat of mortar or fine concrete, about half an inch to an inch thick, so as to produce a level surface ; and then facing that with fine plaster mixed with hair, about $\frac{1}{8}$ inch thick, on which the painting was executed. The colours were laid on while the plaster was wet, and even while it could still be moved by the brush. The long lines of the design were marked by stretching a string, and pressing it upon the still soft plaster. After painting, the whole surface was polished and water-proofed, as seen on a portion which was well protected. Owing to exposure to the weather in the ruined state, it is in every degree of decay : some still perfect, and some spongy and rotted, with all the colours vanished. Most of it was more or less spongy, and the colours liable to be rubbed off. I removed the last coat of earth therefore myself, and then soaked the face with tapioca water. This needed to be thick and gelatinous on the most rotted parts, and scarcely more than mere water on the hardest portions ; the rule being to use it as thick as possible, provided it shall all sink in, and leave the surface just dry. In this way as much as possible is lodged in the pores, while there is no surplus on the face which would be liable to peel off, and remove the colour with it. All the surface—about 300 square yards—was spread with solution by

the finger, as any brush would be liable to rub up the colours.

The first painted pavement, which was found a few days after beginning work, is, P. I, in the south-east hall of columns in the *harem*, where I was digging to search for the pieces of glazed tile from the columns, which I found lying about there. So soon as I knew the limits of that room, I applied to the Government to protect it by a building; and while that building was in progress we found the second chamber, P. 2, near it, after clearing the cubicles and advancing southwards. This was then included in another room, along with the remaining part of pavement 3. It was well that the discovery was made so early in the season, as the various operations of building, roofing, &c., took some months, and needed constant watching to prevent the men injuring the buried pavements over which they worked. The wall between pavements 2 and 3 was levelled down to afford a platform space for visitors to walk along. I made and placed a continuous platform of wood, raised from the floor, so that visitors on entering the building at I can circulate around both chambers, and view the whole without retracing their way. As the moving of wood, and carpentering, over such a delicate surface could not be trusted to any native, I did all that work myself; but I set the best of my boys—Ali Suefi—to put plaster necking round all the broken edges, which he did excellently.

24. Turning now to the details of the paintings. The painted pavement, P. 2, which is in the best condition, is shewn as far as the western half in PL. II. The eastern half was done by an inferior artist, and, as I had not time to copy the whole, I did the western part first. The stone bases of pillars remain in the three north-east places, but all the rest have been dug out anciently for stone, breaking up the pavement around. The sites of the bases are marked by circles on the plan, the white around them being the destroyed parts. It will be seen that the design is a middle passage across the room, marked out by a row of bound captives, alternately Asiatic and Negro, laid on the floor to be trodden under foot; and on either side of the passage a tank of fish surrounded by the columns; then groups of plants and animals between the columns; then a long line of plants and animals beyond the columns; and lastly a border around the room composed of alternate bouquets of lotus, and bowls placed on stands, with their contents garlanded. The small scale plan, PL. II, was reduced by using a frame of threads laid over the painting: hence it is

correct as to spacing; but as the figures were drawn so small, it will be better to judge of the style from the coloured drawings of groups, PLS. III, IV, which were drawn full size, and are reduced photographically.

The artist who did the eastern half of the room was far inferior to the other. Two groups of his work are copied in PL. III, 1, 2; it will be seen that there is less coherence and skill in arranging his plants, the wings of the birds are more clumsy, and the calves are much stiffer and worse in drawing. On the other hand he tried to compensate for his inferiority by more variety. He alone uses the convolvulus, and the insects—locusts, butterflies, and dragon-flies—scattered among the birds; and in the calves he has turned the heads, and made an unhappy attempt at novelty.

The western half of the room shews a fine and firm hand throughout; and, so far as we yet know, this artist was the first man who ever represented rapid motion and instantaneous attitudes. His success must be judged from his starting-point, and not by the results of those who have followed in successive ages beyond his aims. The young bull bounding in the air (III, 3) is well conceived, and only falls short in minor details: the spirit and pose of the whole shews close observation and a memory for motion. The gentle gallop of the calf (IV, 4) is gracefully done, and is far different from the run-away action of the other calf (IV, 5). The plants shew the same naturalism as the animals; the free branching overlapping of the shoots, and the grace of the curves, especially in the group of *Cyperus* and *Arundo* in IV, 6, were a new departure in Egyptian work. At the right hand base of group IV, 5, there is a small portion of a previous pavement, which had become worn, and was broken up to lay the present floor. This is rather different in style, the fish being smaller, and done entirely in grey outline; it indicates a renewal probably within a few years, and belongs to an entirely different plan of design for the floor.

It is noticeable that there are not any geometrical ornaments, nor indeed any conventional forms, in the whole of these designs. In place of the rigid patterns which are often found in Egyptian work, or the stiff rosettes or circles of the Babylonian, there are here only figures of actual objects; and the less flowing border which is needed to go next to the walls, is achieved by copying the bouquets and vases which were familiar in every great house. There is thus a strong presumption against either the style or the artists having come from Babylonia, or from any country where geometrical ornament prevailed. Further, we learn that the artist was a trained Egyptian. In the group IV, 5, he has drawn a thistle with admirable freedom of the branching; while beside it is a lotus plant with all the formality of the stiffest Egyptian. If one plant was naturally varied, why not the other? Here his education is seen. He had been brought up to draw the stock subject, the lotus, and he could not see it otherwise; whereas on plants to which he had not been trained, he threw his full attention for true copying. It appears then that this artist was a native trained Egyptian, not imitating any other school, but under a strong impulse toward naturalism. It should be noted that the black border, around the blue tank of fish and lotus, represents the black mud of the soil; whereas the plants have a yellow band beneath them indicating the sand. The shade lines in the drawing are here used for the heraldic colours, when the figures are viewed upright in each part.

25. The other principal painted floor is in the hall. P. 1; of most of this I made a copy in colour on a scale of 1 : 10, before the building was decided on; but it is not here reproduced as it is in worse state than other pavement, and is of the same style. The plan of it was with a passage way, painted with bound captives, like the other hall; but instead of being straight it enters in the middle of the south side, goes down the middle of the hall, and then turns at right angles to pass out of the west door into hall 3 (see plan, PL. XXXVI). This pathway occupies the middle space between pillars; and the other space on either side between the pillars is painted with a long fish tank. Groups of plants and birds fill the short spaces from pillar to pillar; and a border of bouquets and vases surrounds the room. It seems to have been painted by the inferior artist, from the want of skill in grouping the plants, the use of a favourite bush of his (which is at the right hand end of PL. III, 2), and the stiffness of the animals. He has introduced a yellow lion springing upon one of the bounding calves, facing it and seizing it on the back of the neck. This hall was entered from a corridor P at a slightly higher level, which was also painted, with a border pattern. The hall 3 is painted with plants like 1 and 2; but very little remains of it, and that is much decayed.

Other painted floors exist in the small chambers marked P, of the block of building some way south of the *harem.* They are of the same style, with plants and calves, and what remains is in bad condition;

having been disabled from going about during my last six weeks at this place, I was prevented from finally clearing and copying them.

The colours used for this work are entirely mineral. The blues and greens are all of artificial frits, like the other samples of this period; the reds are burnt yellow ochres, and the yellows raw yellow ochres (the samples of these colours that were found in the town, I ground up to colour my copies on paper); and the black is doubtless soot, from the fineness of it. The use of half tints and shading off of the colours is frequent, on the calves, the birds, and the fishes.

26. Wall painting was also largely used. In the hall, P. 2, the east wall was still high enough to shew part of a design above the dado. The usual dado was of the old panel pattern, generally painted in red, blue, and white. Above that, about 30 inches from the ground, there ran a continuous band of figures. These were not, as in Greek work, grouped closely together; but rather like a story book, with each person in separate action, and yet all connected by one motive. The only continuous group that remained was the long scene in PL. V, which shews exactly the original spacing. The best figures of that scene are given below on a larger scale to shew their details. The story is that of the master returning home, and the preparations for him. At the left is the open door of the house, to shew that the house affairs begin there. Then comes a servant sweeping up the floor with a palm-leaf brush; then the steward hurrying in with his baton; followed by the cook, hot, and wigless from the kitchen, bearing two stands with bowls, which contain a joint of meat and some cakes; following him - is the servant sprinkling the floor, and the contrast is excellent between his easy-going face and the bustle of the cook with little pursed-up lips. Further on we see the great bowls of grapes, garlanded over, which stood near the front door in the entrance; by them is the *bowab* or porter with his great stick, and a messenger has hurriedly come up to tell him that the master is coming; for round the corner of the room, on the south wall, were the feet of the prancing horses which drew the chariot. Thus the corner, dividing between the two walls, was neatly made use of to divide between the indoor and outdoor action. These figures were all painted directly on mud plaster; and the white ants having eaten out every trace of straw from it, and tunnelled it all to pieces, it was impossible to attempt to move the paintings, as they were really on mere dust, held

together by a wash of colour, and pierced in all directions by the prickly roots of the *halfa* grass. Within a few hours of being cleared they began to crumble away while I copied them. Some few fragments I succeeded in moving and soaking in wax, and they just serve to vouch for the character of the work ; but only my being on the spot, and copying this full size at once, has preserved any record of it. Near it were two excellent figures of another scene, shewing a man sitting on a low block, looking up to a servant, who stands talking and gesticulating before him with the dusting brush tucked under his left arm ; of this I have only a reduced copy. These paintings reached within an inch or two of the denuded surface of the ground ; and as all the rest of the room was more denuded, no trace of paintings remained on the other walls.

Another painting was on the east wall of the court of the *harem*. This represented a lake, lotus plants, an overseer and servants with cattle, a winding canal and boats sailing on it, the shores being painted black to shew Nile mud. Only the lower part of this was left, and that in bad state; but I copied it in colour on a reduced scale.

On the wall of the passage, between the doors of the cubicles, were traces of paintings, a box with the regular sloping lid, painted in black and white on a red ground, and five jars painted in red on a yellow ground.

27. Of other wall-paintings we found some portions in house 13 (see map, PL. XXXV, and plan, PL. XL), which is the largest building in the town, after the palace and temples. The best piece was on the wall marked "painting." It was executed on a wash of white plastering, and hence had some coherence on the face, although the back was reduced to dust by the white ants. It was in such brilliant condition that I took particular care to remove it. Fetching large box-lids and sheets of paper, I cut away and broke up the bricks of the wall from behind, without in the least shaking the mud face ; so that at last (as there was no wind that day) the mass of crumbling earth and dust with the painting stood upright in the air, and only held by the one edge and base. The edge was half cut through as I proceeded ; so that when I placed a box-lid against the face, and grasped the fresco and lid together, I could safely turn the lid down horizontal with the fresco lying on it, face downwards. In this way the pieces were transferred for removal to my hut. Then by making frames of bars of wood, and coating these with a paste of mud

and sand, I could press them on the back, so as to give a perfectly equal bearing for the painting ; and on turning over the box-lid and frame, the painting was left attached to the latter, face upwards. With thin board lashed on to the face, padded with wool, I succeeded in transporting these fresco fragments to England without the least loss or injury.

The subject of the best piece was the king seated, life-size (of which the chair and feet remained) ; the queen was seated facing him (of which only the cushion and feet remained) ; attendants between them of small size (the lower half of which remained) ; and two complete figures of the little princesses seated on cushions by the queen's side. Owing to their small size and low position they were preserved entire, excepting for a little damage by fallen bricks. They are shewn in PL. I, 12. The expression is admirable ; the patronising air of the elder sister chucking the little one under the chin, and the self-possession with which she rests her arm on her drawn-up knees, contrasts with the helpless look of the younger one, half-supported by her hands. The limbs and bodies shew a distinct use of dark shading toward the edges, while the high lights on the skin are indicated by dusting the surface with fine powder of orpiment, which gives a glitter without altering the actual flesh colour used. This is perhaps the only instance of the use of light and shade by Egyptians ; and it shews that if this school had not come to an untimely end, it might have developed realistic painting.

The other pieces on the walls of this house were the legs of two kneeling captives (Asiatic and Negro), with a bowl on a stand between them, and the legs of some figures and a flight of stairs ; many chips of fresco were found fallen from the walls, shewing ornamented coffers, groups of faces, &c. Doubtless many more frescoes and more perfect ones might have been obtained from here, if the walls had not been pulled to pieces in recent years to get bricks for the Arab village.

28. When I first went to Tell el Amarna, I aimed at finding the rubbish heaps, where the waste was thrown from the palace. I searched all around the palace region, but could not find any such remains ; while clearing, however, on the desert, about three furlongs from the palace, I found a wide stretch of waste heaps. As they are on the nearest open ground to the palace, and contained scattered throughout the whole area dozens of objects with the names of the royal family, and hundreds of pieces of imported Aegean pottery, it seems evident that these are the

palace waste heaps which I sought; though probably mixed with waste from other large houses in the neighbourhood. The extent of the heaps was about 600 feet by 400 feet, and the depth varied from 4 feet to a mere sprinkling, probably averaging more than 1 foot. The whole of this was turned over, and the lads and boys employed were encouraged to preserve everything beyond the rough pottery.

Nearly all the broken rings, &c., with cartouches that I obtained, were found here; these comprised a few of Tahutmes III and Amenhotep III (doubtless brought here), and about 80 or 90 of Akhenaten, his family, and his successor, Ra-smenkh-ka; on most of the latter, however, he called himself "beloved of Akhenaten," and they date, therefore, during a co-regency, or soon after Akhenaten's death, when his successor still trusted to his name for support. Thus it is clear that the mounds belong to a very little longer time than the reign of Akhenaten; and as he only reigned here for twelve years, everything found in the mounds was probably thrown away within fifteen years, at about 1400 B.C. Strange to say, several scattered human bones were found among the pottery, a radius, ribs, &c., which did not belong to any burial, but had been thrown there with the pot-sherds.

29. The principal importance of these mounds was quite unexpected. So soon as we began to dig we found Aegean pottery and so-called Phoenician glass; and the quantities of pieces of these materials prove how usual they were at the time. The glass vases were of many patterns, as yet quite unknown; but, from the factories of glass-working found here, it is almost certain that they were made on the spot, as we shall notice in the chapter IV on manufactures. Every piece with visible pattern was preserved, and the total amount is 750 pieces from the rubbish mounds, 38 from the palace, and none from elsewhere. The next question is, How many vases does this heap represent? A dozen types were so peculiar that every piece of them could be easily selected, and apparently all the pieces of each of these types had come from one vase. Then measuring the area of the pieces of one type, and estimating from the curvature the size of the whole vase, it is easy to see what proportion of each vase is represented by the chips found here. It is remarkably small, never as much as one quarter, and often only a hundredth; all the rest must have been thrown elsewhere, probably into the river with the kitchen waste, while a few bits went into the dust-hole, to be brought out here with the solid stuff and

potsherds. The average on the dozen vases is one-twelfth of each vase, or five chips out of each. Hence the 750 chips would represent about 150 glass vases originally; a large number considering the general value and rarity of such, and quite enough to come as broken waste from a palace in fifteen years. The type specimens are in the glass department of the British Museum, and will perhaps be published in "Archaeologia."

30. The Aegean pottery is however more important, as there is no indication that it was ever made in Egypt; and its presence therefore shews the coeval civilization of the Aegean countries with which it is always associated. The total quantity of pieces found was 1329 in the waste heaps, 9 in the palace, and only 3 fragments of one vase elsewhere, in house 11. Selecting vases which are of distinctly individual patterns, and cannot be confounded with any other pieces, there are 45 fragments representing 28 vases, so that on the average there is not even two pieces from a vase. This indicates that the 1341 pieces would have been derived from the destruction of over 800 vases.

The number of fragments, and percentage of the whole, is as follow:

			Pieces.	Per cent.
Pyxides	. . .	(Pl. XXVI., 1–10)	51	4
Bowls	. . .	(,, 11–15)	15	1
Piriform, wide neck	.	(,, 16–25)	50	4
Piriform, white line	.	(XXVII., 26–34)	7	$\frac{1}{2}$
Piriform	. . .	(,, 30, 31)	477	$35\frac{1}{2}$
False necks, piriform?	(XXVIII., 35–77)		136	10
(Total piriform	.	. . .	670	50)
Globular	. (Pl. XXIX, XXX., 78–143)		569	42
Conchoidal pattern	. . . . .		24	2
Thick, matt face	. . . .		12	1
			1341	100
Cypriote	. . . . . .		3	
Phoenician	. . . . .		81	6
			1425	

The term *piriform* is here used for those vases, most commonly found at Ialysos, in Rhodes, which have a wide shoulder, and thence taper in a long slope to a narrow base. The top is either a wide neck, large enough for the hand (18), or else a false neck (37); and hence the false necks when found alone have no clear indication whether they belong to *piriform* vases, or to the flatter types common at Mykenae, which are even as low as only half a diameter in height. Here I have classed all the false necks as piriform vases, because other portions of piriform vases are abundant, while there has not been a single piece found clearly belonging to the flatter, lower, type of false-necked vases.

The character of the vases found here has an important bearing on the nature of the trade at that period. We see that half the Aegean ware is of piriform vases, which are most commonly found in Rhodes, and nearly the other half is of globular vases, which are peculiarly Cypriote; the balance, only 8 per cent. of the whole, is not distinctive of any other locality, and there is no type specially Mykenaean. Hence it seems that the trade was with the south of Asia Minor, rather than with the Greek peninsula. Further, there is very little that is characteristic of the Phoenicians; the black-brown Phoenician ware is but 6 per cent. of the quantity of Aegean, and the Cypriote bowls—hemispherical white with brown stitch pattern—are scarcely known. Hence the trade does not seem so likely to have been carried on by land, or through Semitic or Phoenician connections, as through the race or races who made and used the Aegean pottery.

The plates (XXVI to XXX) shew all the distinctive pieces of patterns that were found. The pyxis form (1–10) is always straight-sided, and generally flat-bottomed. The bowls (11–15) are not usual. 11 has three incised lines around the outside, forming a sort of moulding; at first this looks like a piece of Samian, but the paste and the bands inside are clearly Aegean; the more upright bowls or cups (13–15) are of the earlier Aegean period. The wide-necked piriform vases are patterned with lines, simple or crossing (16–25); and it is not certain whether the white-patterned piriform vases were wide-necked or false-necked. This use of white line belongs to the earlier age of Aegean ware. The false necks (35–77) belong probably to piriform vases, as many such bases are found. The globular vases are all made on a vertical axis, and differ therefore from the pilgrim bottles, which are similarly ornamented; the decoration is, however, put on by turning the vase on a horizontal axis. These seem to be rather more advanced in decoration than the piriform vases, as there is the lotus, 103, 104, 108, 121–6; an ivy leaf, 106; and plants, 107, 138.

The absence of certain types from the large quantity of many hundreds of vases which have furnished this mass of fragments, is worth notice. There are none of the small false-necked vases of flat, low, form, which are the commonest at Gurob; there are no hydriae and no animal figures, both of which are found at Gurob. In short, the impression is that this pottery belongs to an entirely different trade

route to that of Gurob; that this came down with the Syrian coasting vessels from Cyprus and Rhodes, while the Gurob Aegean ware belongs rather to Greece, and came along the African coast to the Fayum.

31. It is almost needless to observe that this discovery and dating of Aegean pottery stands on an entirely different footing to those which have been previously made in Egypt and Greece. All previous correlations have depended on single vases, or on single scarabs found associated with things from other sources; and hence (to any one without a practical knowledge of how completely things are of one period, in almost all cases when they are associated), it may seem as if the dating all depended on isolated objects, any of which might have been buried centuries after it was made. Here we have not to consider isolated objects, about which any such questions can arise, nor a small deposit which might be casually disturbed, nor a locality which has ever been reoccupied; but we have to deal with thousands of tons of waste heaps, with pieces of hundreds of vases, and about a hundred absolutely dated objects with cartouches. And when we see that in all this mass, which is on a scale that is beyond any possibility of accidental or casual mixture throughout, there is not a single object which can be dated later than about 1380 B.C., we may henceforward remember that there are few facts in all archaeology determined with a more overwhelming amount of evidence than the dating of this earlier style of Aegean pottery to the beginning of the fourteenth century B.C.

32. On the plan (PL. XXXV) will be seen, just west of the great temple, a site marked " Ushabtis." Here was found a cast, taken from the face of Akhenaten, after death (see Frontispiece). The attribution of this, and the details of it, will be discussed in chapter VIII, on the Historical Results. But this led to another discovery. On clearing the ground about there, which was only covered by about a foot of sand, we found several unfinished ushabti figures in various stones, all accidentally broken in the course of roughing them out; some were of red granite, some black granite, some hard limestone. Such granite ushabtis are very unusual; but as the ushabtis of Akhenaten, found in his tomb, are of red and black granite, it seems highly probable that this working of granite ushabtis just at the end of the palace, was for the manufacture of the royal tomb furniture. At the same spot was a great quantity of granite dust, resulting from the working of granite on a large scale;

and if these ushabtis were for Akhenaten's tomb, his granite sarcophagus was doubtless worked here also. The purpose of making the cast of his head after death is also obvious, as it would be needed for making correct images for his *ka*, and as a model for the inner coffin of wood and the ushabtis. Other pieces of sculptors' trial work in different materials were also found in this place.

33. The Great Temple occupies a large space, nearly half a mile long (PL. XXXVII). And though the temple proper only covers a small fraction of the space, at one end of the area, yet the whole length is strewn with fragments of stonework ; and we know from the views in the tombs, how rows of altars stood on either side of the road to the shrine. The site of the temple, or shrine, which was entirely excavated by Mr. Carter, is marked by heaps of broken pieces of mortar and stone ; and the cores of the walls consisting of mortar and chips still remain to shew the position. Mr. Carter turned over nearly all of this without finding anything more than two or three blocks of the great stele. This was built up of small blocks, and bore a life-size figure of Akhenaten (of which the head was found), and doubtless similar figures of the queen and princesses, whose titles were also found (PL. VIII).

34. The absence of all sculptures was partly explained on searching the heap which lay just outside of the temenos wall, on the south of the temple. Here were found portions of seventeen limestone statues of the king and queen, probably those which are represented in porticoes in the drawing of the temple. The identifiable remains of these statues, beside about a ton of fragments, are as follow :—

Akhenaten.

1. Cap, neck and shoulders, pieces of chest with Aten names, 2 hands with an offering slab, leg. Life size. Good stone, fine work, dry finish.
2. Cap and pier, mouth, shoulder, bit of side. Nearly double life size. Good stone, fine work.
3. Cap, 2 bits of head, most of torso with Aten names. Over life size. Medium stone and work.
4. Cap, 2 ears and cheek. Half more than life size.
5. Cap, mouth, nose, ear, and neck. Over ? life size. Good stone and work.
6. Cap and most of head, neck. Over ? life size. Good stone, fair work.
7. Cap and most of head, scrap of mouth. Life size. Good stone, fair work.

8. Smooth wig, top front of head, bits of beard and chest. Over ? life size. Medium stone and work.
9. Smooth wig, most of the head, chest with Aten names. Under life size. Medium stone and work.
10. Ribbed head-dress, half head, bit of chest with Aten names. Life size. Good stone, fair work.
11. Ribbed head-dress. Piece of lappet, and tail of cloth, one shoulder. Small size. Bad stone, fair work.
12. Ribbed head-dress, and ear, scraps. About life size. Medium stone, scanty work.

Nefert-ythi.

13. Short wig. Bits of head, torso. Nearly life size. Medium stone and work.
14. Plain wig, inscription on back.
15. Plain wig, inscription on back, mouth and nose (PL. I, 15). Finest stone and work.
16. Lappet wig, two bits, shoulder, breast.
17. Torso (PL. I, 13). With back pier, nose, feet, throne. Nearly life size. Finest stone and work.

A head of Akhenaten, probably from one of these statues, was found by Perring, and is now in the British Museum. The stone varies from a brilliant hard, semi-crystalline limestone, to a softer and more porous variety ; but it is in all cases far superior to the soft chalky limestone used for building. This harder stone is found in the neighbouring hills ; and was selected for the site of stele S, which is in as perfect condition as when carved. The steles on softer rock have weathered largely, and those of Tuneh (the western bank) being on nummulitic limestone have also been mostly effaced.

Beside these life-size statues in the temple, there were also colossal standing figures of Akhenaten, in soft limestone, of which an ear, a toe, and a piece of the chest were found. The attitude seems to have been with crossed arms holding the crook and flail, but whether standing (like an osirian figure or ushabti), or seated (like his statue in the Louvre) is not determined.

Among the fragments of the statues were also pieces of tablets, inscribed on the front with the cartouches of the Aten, and on the sides with those of the king. On one of these the position of the hands carved below it, point out that it was held by a kneeling figure, presenting it in the usual posture of offering:

the tablet resting on one hand, and being steadied by the other hand behind it.

Other similar tablets, made of blue-glazed pottery in high relief, were perhaps placed in the hands of other statues. A large tablet of fine limestone with the Aten and royal cartouches is in the Turin Museum; but as it is 42 inches high and 30 wide it is too large for a statue, and was therefore an independent offering in the temple. The finely carved stele of PL. XII, I, is in the finest crystalline limestone; it was also found in the temple. Outside of the temenos, in the heap of rubbish with the statues, were many pans of red pottery, containing resin melted in and pieces of charcoal. These appear to be the pans used for burning incense in the temple, which were thrown aside when done with.

35. Beside the shrine at the east end of the enclosure, there were several large buildings near the entrance, at the west end. The principal remains are two great masses of concrete, each 62 feet 9 inches × 29 feet 1 inch, and about 8 feet deep, shaded diagonally in the plan (PL. XXXVII). Around them is the mark of an empty space varying from 28 to 36 inches wide, from which a stone foundation has been extracted (marked black and white in plan); and sand lies beyond that out to 52 or 110 inches from the block (left white). A brick wall (marked black) surrounds and retains this sand. Between these foundations lie another hollow trench and a concrete way. It appears as if there had existed two blocks of building each 68 × 34 feet, or 40 × 20 cubits, and a roadway 25 feet 7 inches, or 15 cubits, between them. The cubit resulting by this, from centre to centre of the blocks (so as to be clear from the uncertainty of the casing thickness), would be 20·57 inches. The corners of the blocks are recessed 51 or 54 × 109 or 110 inches, probably to receive an extra mass of masonry at the corners. This form is exactly like the great blocks of brickwork of about two-thirds of this size, which from their position must have supported a gateway at the side of the palace (PL. XXXVI); and it seems therefore that this must have been a great gateway of approach to the temple. It is not like the Egyptian pylon as that is always broader on the face than the depth of it. Here, on the contrary, the face is much less than the depth, like the piers of a Roman archway.

Within this are masonry remains of square pillars, rough on the face, and built of small blocks. As these vary from 36 to 45 inches in the side, and are only 20 to 27 inches apart, they are clearly a sub-

structure. They might have supported large columns; but that is not likely, as they are only 5 feet centre to centre, so there is no room for even the 18-inch columns of the *harem*; but, more probably they bore the corners of paving slabs 5 feet square, which flagged a great hall or court situated here.

On the south of the entrance was a great forest of pillars of brick, like that south of the palace. These pillars are smaller than those in the hall of the palace, the pillar and space together averaging 113 inches east to west, and 121 inches north to south. I began by discovering and clearing those near the gateway, and gradually extended the clearance until about 15 or 20 rows were bared. As nothing of interest was found in the depth of a yard or more of earth, I then prospected for the next, and traced them by sample out as far east as they are drawn, 36 rows in all. At that point they were denuded down to only an inch or two, and all beyond that has been entirely denuded away, so that we cannot know how far this hall originally extended.

These enormous halls are a new feature at Tell el Amarna. No such forests of pillars are known in earlier times in Egypt, and it was as much an invention as any other branch of the architecture. But we see in these the prototype of the great hall of columns at Karnak. These halls contained over five hundred or a thousand pillars; while that of Karnak is more massive, but far less extensive, and contains 150 columns.

36. The rough plan placed by the side of the temple plan on PL. XXXVII is all that can now be obtained from a document of great interest. About 1885 Prof. Sayce found a plan of a building drawn in the quarry at Tell el Amarna; he made a rough copy, and intended to re-visit it, but on his going there in 1892 the whole of that part of the quarry had been blasted away. This drawing is made from that which he noted down, which is the only record of this design. He describes its position as being on the south side of the quarry a little to the north of the wely at Shekh Said. It was drawn in yellow colour lengthways on the wall, about 8 feet long and 2 feet high, at about 5½ feet from the ground. It appears to be a working design for some great building. The number of architraves in the length of it is 29 short and 2 long. If the pillars were as close as those in the passage of the *harem* this would imply a length of 250 feet, or if as large as those in the hall of columns then it would be 450 long. Now the shrine of the Great Temple was not 200 feet long, and this

plan would be unsuited for a temple. There may have been a building within the great gate of the temple, but if this had been there we should see more chips and mortar and concrete lying about. It cannot be referred to the smaller temple, by its length. And on looking at the palace plan (PL. XXXVI) we see only one place where the foundations could correspond to such a building; that is in the space marked Q, with the front towards the river westwards; but, if so, half of the area is now under cultivation. This seems hardly a probable site, as I did not find any pieces of columns in all this region. So it may belong to a building entirely under the cultivated land, or it may be a sketch that was never carried out.

CHAPTER III.

THE HOUSES.

37. So little is yet known about the system of Egyptian houses, that a series of house plans—such as we now have from Tell el Amarna—deserves careful study. There are particular advantages in working on these houses, rather than on those of ordinary Egyptian towns. They were all built in one generation, and can therefore be properly compared together, and only shew contemporary variations of design, and not changes of fashion. They were never rebuilt, and but little altered, owing to the brief occupation of the site. They were laid out on open desert, free from obstructions, and with ample space, as most of them are in enclosures; much like the little villas which are dotted about the edge of the desert near Matarieh at present. There are the same advantages that we had in the study of Kahun, which was all laid out at once, and which shews by the exact resemblance between houses of the same size that the architect gave certains designs to be repeated as often as required (see " Illahun," PL. XIV). Here at Tell el Amarna the conditions were rather different; the quality of the houses is intermediate between the mansions of the nobles, and the streets of the workmen which constituted the town of Kahun A large middle-class bureaucracy demanded villas of a moderate size, and different modifications of the same general elements were made in various instances.

In each period different requirements must have led to varying types of house, as is the case in every other country. The distribution of wealth in different classes is reflected in the differences between Kahun and Tell el Amarna; the absence of middle-class houses in the former, the prevalence of them in the latter place. The position of women mainly controls the arrangement of a house; the separation of men and women servants, needed where there were no private sleeping rooms for inferiors, is the main condition in ancient Egypt; while the strict *harem* system of modern Islam was quite unknown, and the elements and terms of a modern Arab house cannot be applied to denote the divisions of the ancient houses.

The houses now excavated were selected for their good condition, and their isolation from the interference of other buildings. They proved remarkably bare of antiquities; not a single piece of papyrus, and scarcely even a potsherd was found in any of them, nor were any buried deposits found, although the floors were all searched for soft or broken places. It is evident that the town had been gradually deserted; and the remaining inhabitants had cleared out from each house, when it was abandoned, every object that could be of any possible use. Hence there is nothing left in place, except some stone tanks, and bases of columns, to throw light on the purposes of the rooms.

38. We will begin by dividing the houses into their various elements. Each house on the plans (PLS. XXXVIII–XXXIX) is numbered separately 1 to 11, and each room of the same nature is marked with the same letter; thus analogous parts can always be seen at a glance by the recurrence of the letters. The most regular house for study is No. 6, which we may consider as the typical example, from which the others are variations. All plans are with the approximate north upwards on the page; this is really between 15° and 30° E. of N. in most of the town.

The approach to the house, A, was often up a flight of shallow steps (as in 4, 5, 6), when the house stood on a raised platform a foot or two above the plain. This approach led along one side of the house, most usually the north, sometimes east or west, but never south. It led up to a room which always looks down the steps, or way, and is extraneous to the house proper. This room, marked P, is doubtless the place of the porter or door-keeper; and it was very likely open at the sides, with a roof supported on posts or small pillars.

Entering the actual house, there is always a lobby, marked Y, at the end of the summer room, or *Loggia*, L, into which it leads. This, Y, was probably a place for leaving superfluous dress, and outdoor objects; where also the door-keeper would sleep. The loggia,

L, is always on the north side of the house, and in one case, No. 4, where the entrance required the loggia to be on the west, there was a second loggia provided on the north as well. The loggia is also defended by smaller rooms at each end, so that three sides of it could never be heated by the sun ; and in some cases the north side was also protected by the projecting porter's-room, P (see Nos. 5, 6, 8). It is evident that this was for a cool room facing north, and probably open along the north front, with the roof supported by pillars ; in fact a kind of verandah. Owing to this being an outer wall of the house it is always much denuded, and no trace of the upper parts of it remain to shew the arrangement. At the end of this are usually two small rooms, O, Q (Nos. 3, 4, 7, 8, 9), or sometimes but one (Nos, 2, 6, 10) ; as these open on the most public part of the house they were probably occasional rooms for visitors or strangers.

The most permanent part of the design was the square hall, H, in the centre of the whole house. This appears to have been the general sitting-room, especially for winter use. It often has a low raised bench or *mastaba* along one side, and in front of that (see Nos. 4, 6, 21) was the fire, near the middle of the hall, to warm those who sat on the *mastaba*. There was no central opening in the roof, as the column is generally in the middle of the room ; but in one case (No. 6) there are two columns. Probably it was lighted mainly from the wide doorway facing the open side of the loggia. Some difference of level in the roofing by the staircase may easily have given any more light that was needed. A single square foot of sky-view will easily light a large room in Egypt.

39. A feature of the hall which is quite unaccountable at present is the red recess, which occurs in several houses (Nos. 1, 2, 5, 9, 10). This is a flat recessed strip of the wall, sometimes with an inner recess within it, much like the old "false-door" of the tombs. But in no case was any top found, though in No. 9 it remained still about 5 or 6 feet high. It appears then as if it ran nearly the whole height of the room. It is always smoothly plastered with the usual mud plaster, and painted bright haematite red. There is never any trace of ornament, or inscription, or figure ; not even a border-line. Nor is there any hollow in the wall behind it, nor any space or difference in the floor in front of it. It is not constant in position, occurring thrice on the west, twice on the south, once east, but never north : and it has no constant relation to the other chambers. The widths

of the recesses are (2) 25 in 41 ; (5) 25 in 41, and 27 in 41 ; (9) 33 in 51 ; (10) 23 inches.

40. The body of the house, after these public rooms, divides into four groups, which are always quite distinct from each other. These are B–G the master's room and women's quarter ; I–K the men's quarter ; M, N, store rooms, and S–V the staircase and cupboards. In each house is one peculiar room, C, with a somewhat narrower portion, which is always at the south end of it ; the narrow portion is diminished by a thickening of the walls, and the floor of this part is also slightly raised. This would seem to be the master's sleeping room, with the raised portion for the bed place. In every case this room, C, opens out of a branching room, B, which leads both to C, and to a number of small offices, D, E, F, G. Of these D is a side room opening off B and not leading elsewhere. The use of all these rooms is apparently for cooking, etc., judging from where we find them most developed, as in Nos. 4 and 9 ; and they never lead outside of the house. From these features they are probably the women's household rooms, and D the women's sleeping room. Being always to the south side, the prevalent north wind would not blow the heat and smell of cooking into the house.

41. The other main group is I, J, K. Of these I is always a large square room, or secondary hall ; often with a central pillar, and nearly as large as the main central hall. This set of rooms, I, J, K, never has any connection with the set B–G or women's rooms, except in one case in No. 9 where I opens into the passage or branching room B. But I, J, K, in three cases have a back door out of the house, in No. 5 opening on to the loggia in place of an occasional room, in No. 9 leading to an outer court with granaries, and in No. 11 opening on the approach, but blocked up later on. Hence from those features it seems that this was the men's quarter ; I being the common hall for the servants, and the other rooms being sleeping rooms, perhaps for the married men, and sometimes leading outside.

42. In the next section are the rooms M, N, perhaps for stores and goods, equal to the modern *Khazneh* in Egypt. They always open from the central hall H, have no connection, and are opposite to the staircase. The last section is the staircase, S, leading to the roof, with sundry rooms and cupboards, T, U, V, fitted in according to the space left to spare on this side of the hall. The arrow in each plan points upward. In No. 3 the stair was winding, and ran over two cupboards, T, U. In No. 5 the stair turned over a long

recess, which opened beneath it ; and T appears to be a separate room. In No. 6 the stair ran over a dumb hollow, and over the small room U branching from T. In 9 the stair is reached by a branch from the loggia, and went in one flight on to the top of the hall, judging by the height to which it attains as it now stands. In No. 10 the stair winds around a square pillar, and had a winding cupboard, T, beneath it. In No. 7 there was probably a wooden stair, of which nothing now remains, fitted in the long narrow passages. Thus in four houses the stair is on the east, and in two on the west, but never north or south.

Amid all the variety of these houses, of which no two are alike, and which appears quite irregular at first sight, we nevertheless see that six entirely separate classes of rooms may be observed ; the characters of these rooms, and their relation to, or isolation from, the others is constant ; and from their peculiarities we may trace their uses with scarcely a possibility of a different conclusion.

43. We will now observe the peculiarities of some houses which depart from the normal type.

No. 1 has been greatly denuded around, and probably an outer wall has been removed for the sake of the bricks. At first sight it seems as if it might be open chambers with merely a verandah or long eaves around ; and this may possibly be the case, as it is only half brick thick, as slight as possible, and was perhaps run up for a temporary house while building a more regular mansion. Only the hall and loggia are regular, and the rest of it seems to be merely for men and stores, without a master's room or other usual features.

No. 2 is much simplified from the full type ; but yet nearly all the regulation divisions can be seen.

No. 3 is irregular in having no separate master's room and *harem*, nor men's rooms. It may be therefore a secondary house for receiving guests, and not for a household.

Nos. 4, 5, 6 and 7 all have the usual divisions ; but 6 has a long out-house added on the south wall.

Nos. 8 and 9 are adjacent, with the property divided by a very irregular wall between. 9 has the unusual addition of a large courtyard on a lower level, containing three conical granaries. In this court were found the two fragments of a red jasper foot of a statue.

No. 10 has no regular approach, nor back premises. A large divided court occupies the north front ; and at the back is a very peculiar washing place, E, of which a sketch is given below the plan. It is a small

recess, paved with a slope to the front. Two steps lead up into it. The front is half enclosed with a dwarf wall of stone on edge, so as to give privacy for minor ablutions, and a hole below this wall allowed the waste water to run off into a small tank in front. Such an arrangement is wholly unknown elsewhere ; the dwarf wall shews that it was not for mere dish or clothes washing, but for private ablutions such as Muhamedans now make ; in short, it is exactly the sort of place that Islam requires, and the adjoining recess, D, which could be reached from the stone steps of E without touching ordinary ground, would be just what is needed for a praying place. Is it possible that this—which is in a very abnormal type of house —belonged to a Semitic resident at Akhenaten's court, and·that the practices of Islam have been taken over entire from pre-Muhamedan times? The addition to the house on the east is also abnormal. The hall was probably open in the middle, as the space between the pillars is much longer than usual ; it has three outer doors without any cover. Three long chambers lie south of it ; one reached from the house and two from the hall, one with a raised bench six inches high all around it. The house wall on the north adjoins at the west to a very thick enclosure wall of the whole property.

No. 11 is of the normal type, but has been altered, blocking up the proper entrance to the loggia, and destroying one of the occasional rooms to make a new door.

44. The surroundings of these houses are much alike. An outer wall encloses the property, in the middle of which the house stands. And on the north of each house is a pit in the ground. These pits we frequently dug into, to try to discover their purpose, but no clear result could be obtained. That which I examined most thoroughly was one of the largest, on the north of No. 10. It was cut in clean sand, 12 feet deep, and 12 feet wide. The bottom was flat ; the side had a ledge around it about two feet up, and thence rose steeply to the surface. It was filled with sand, dust, and potsherds thrown in from the house-side of it, and lying in steep strata. There was no sign of other refuse, although bones or skin would have been preserved. It cannot therefore have been for house refuse. Nor from the filling and the size of it could it be for sewage. The only supposition seems to be that they dug the hole for sand, to mix with the Nile mud, in making the mortar for building ; and that then it was filled up with sweepings and broken food-vessels of the workmen. From the hollow now visible

it seems then to have been left as a pit, to catch any heavy rains, and to keep the ground dry by the house. Still it is remarkable that no bones or waste have been found in any of these holes.

45. In the palace, No. 13 (PL. XL), a totally different arrangement appears. This is the largest building in the town, after the great temple and the king's palace, and probably belonged to one of the highest officials. It lies close to the royal palace on the opposite side of the high road. No remains whatever—not even potsherds—were found in the whole extent of the building; and but for the discovery of some fragments of fresco left on the walls it would have been an entire blank, like the other houses. The best painting was in a chamber near the east side, marked "PAINTING" on the plan; only the lower part of a scene remained, all above that having been destroyed when in recent years the people took bricks from here for building the northern village. The scene represented the king seated on a throne, the queen on a divan facing him, attendants between them, and two infant princesses on a cushion at the queen's side. Being the lowest figures in the whole, they were preserved complete; and I succeeded in removing the piece entire, and finally sending it to the Ashmolean Museum, Oxford. A small photograph of the figures is in PL. I, No. 12. The plan of the palace does not shew a single one of the six elements which we have traced in the ordinary houses; and it seems hopeless to ascertain the use of the rooms, until other such buildings may be studied. The room of the painting, and that adjoining it, have curious L-shaped walls of thin brickwork. The introduction of such into a room is unparalleled; and the only use I can guess for them is to support heavy *mulkafs*, or ventilators of wood on the roof, for which the ordinary roofing timbers would not suffice. In this—as in the other houses—the positions of the columns are often only known by the holes left in the floors, where the base stones have been extracted.

46. No. 14 is a large public building which stands on the desert outside of the south end of the town. It is conspicuous by the brick core of one side of the gate remaining still, about 6 feet high, while all the rest is level with the ground; and this mass of black brick is a landmark for a mile or two round. The arrangement is neither suited for a house nor for store rooms. Such large halls seem best adapted for a barrack; and the row of little divisions along the side of the passages are much like the bins found in a passage of the palace, and seem as if for stores of

corn or fodder allotted to about forty different men. The position of the building, beyond the outskirts of the town, and toward the side most exposed to attacks from the desert, makes it reasonable to suppose that it may have been a police barrack of the *mazau;* they were important at Tell el Amarna, situated as it is close to unseen deserts; their patrol paths edge the crests of the hills; and they are shewn in the tomb of their chief at this place, as being stationed in sentry boxes, with a long cord stretched from one to another so that they could signal silently during the night.

47. No. 16 is another large public building, which may well have been for stores, judging by the number of similar chambers.

No. 17 is a series of store rooms on the east of the great house, No. 13, in which the princess fresco was found. They contained nothing but a few of the large clay lumps which sealed the wine jars, with stamps upon them.

No. 18 is another set of store rooms, in which nothing was found except pieces of an alabaster slab with an inscription mentioning Amenhotep III, probably after his death. These rooms were cleared, as they were within about 200 feet of the room which contained the cuneiform tablets; and every possible site within that distance was examined, for the chance of finding another deposit.

48. The cuneiform tablets bearing the royal correspondence with Syria, were found in the block of chambers No. 19 (PLS. XXXV, XLII). From the appearance of the chambers I believe the tablets were in the S.W. room. This site was shewn to Prof. Sayce in a previous year as the place where the tablets were found. Some natives, while I was at Tell el Amarna, offered to shew me a valuable site if I would employ them; I replied, as I always do to such offers, by telling them to go and get something from it, and I would pay them well and employ them. They went and dug in this block of building; I watched them; they found nothing then, as it was exhausted, but this shewed me the spot which they deemed valuable. Afterwards I enquired of a man, where the tablets were found, and he led me to this place. Lastly, when we dug here I found one piece of a tablet in a chamber, and two rubbish-pits, which had been filled up before the walls were built, and which contained the other fragments described and drawn by Prof. Sayce in chapter VI, and PLS. XXXI to XXXIII.

There cannot therefore be any doubt as to the site of this great discovery, which was so lamentably spoilt by the present conditions attaching to such discoveries in Egypt. The tablets were all grubbed out by the fellahin, many were broken, or ground to pieces, during transit on donkey back; the authorities to whom the things were shewn, despised them; and it was very fortunate that the whole discovery was not irrevocably lost. What is saved is but a portion—perhaps not half—of what might have been preserved with proper care.

I searched the site, and all around it, thoroughly. Each of these chambers we dug out down below the walls, until native sand was reached. Thus we descended about 8 feet in parts, and so found the two early rubbish-pits. These proved that the cuneiform scribe lived close by this spot, before the chambers were built to receive the archives. The pieces of tablets which I found are more of them dictionaries and working materials than actual letters. Apparently we have recovered even the very names of the Babylonian scribe and his Egyptian servant, on the little cylinder of clay which he had moulded, perhaps to please the servant who longed to have a cylinder seal like that of his master, as Egyptians now covet a duplicate of anything curious or important. It is inscribed for Tetuna, probably an Egyptian, servant of Samas-niki, which would be the name of the scribe. The fancy for it once past it was thrown into the waste-pit as being useless.

Beside clearing the chambers I cleared all the ground north of them for 200 feet, up to the end of the chamber No. 18. West and south of them was open ground with only a few inches of rubbish over it, which we turned over for the chance of more pits. East of the chambers was a road, and then a house, partly destroyed, No. 21, which I also cleaned out; beyond this were other houses which we cleared, and found one stray piece of a tablet. Thus it is certain now that no other deposit of tablets exists for about 200 feet around the store-rooms.

While digging just south of the cuneiform chambers, No. 19, we found the ground very low, and in the filling up of it were some rolled lumps of desert limestone. These were inscribed in ink, and recorded the boundaries of the plot of ground belonging to an official. The longest inscription is "side, south-east, of the royal scribe Ra-apiy." It is quite possible that this person was the Egyptian scribe of the archives, as the stone evidently belonged to an allotment of land to a royal scribe close to the archive chamber. We see how on laying out the town, the largest handy piece of desert-stone was picked up and inscribed for

a boundary stone, until the plot was walled in; and then it was thrown aside as waste.

The building at Fig. 20, PL. XLII, is a rude walling of loose stone on a platform in front of the northmost stele V. It is most likely that this belongs to a later period, when this vertical face of the stele was selected for one side of a hut, and it is rather of the Roman age than of the period of the stele.

We return now to consider the peculiar structures that we have passed over in describing the houses and store-rooms.

49. No. 15 is a building near the south end of the town. The walls slope down gradually to the north, and it is highest at the south end of the rectangular part, where it is still about ten feet high. Such large circular buildings (for the extraneous buildings at the sides are later additions) seem most like the usual Egyptian granary on a great scale. The use of the long walls to the north, would then be for a sloping way by which the men would walk up to shoot the grain-sacks into the conical granaries on either hand. The circles are 26 feet 6 inches and 29 feet 11 inches inside diameter; the sloping ascent being 100 feet long is not likely to have been under 25 feet high; if then the corn averaged 20 feet high in the granaries they would hold corn enough for three or four thousand men for a year. So this building may well have held the whole of the store for government and official use.

As I have said, the side-chambers are later additions, possibly first added to strengthen the walls. The doorways were cut in the sides, and afterwards roughly blocked up. In each of the four chambers added to the east granary there was a body deposited; one was a boy with the front permanent teeth not through, another a lad yet without wisdom teeth. In the space between the granaries, closed by a short cross wall, was a mixture of bones of men and animals in the earth-filling, some three feet above the ground, and hence deposited when the building had begun to fall into decay.

Lastly there is the remarkable building No. 12. It consists of two circles of brickwork, which were traced all around without finding any opening. As the outer circle, which is over 100 feet across, is still about 4 feet high it is tolerably certain that no entrance ever existed. In the inner circle are two irregular pits lined with brickwork, 5 feet deep. These contained nothing noticeable according to Mr. Carter's examination, except a very rough headrest of limestone; and I picked up a scrap of calcined bone among the earth. The mean diameters of the circles are 430 and 516 inches, and 1215 and 1343 inches.

50. On examining the dimensions of the buildings it seems that a usual plan was to fix on some number of cubits for the hall, and sometimes for the whole house; then the chambers were partly determined by even numbers of cubits, and partly by resultant quantities involving the thickness of the walls.

The bricks varied in size; but they were never even divisions of the cubit, so as to make the walls work in with the cubit. From 12 to 15 inches long, and half as wide was the usual size for bricks. The varieties of the cubit that appear to have been used are, in inches:

20·2	No.	1	20·68	No. 18
20·42	„	2	20·70	„ 5
20·43	„	6	20·70	„ 11
20·56	„	14	20·72	„ 8
20·58	„	17	20·76	„ 10
20·60	„	19	20·77	„ 7
20·62	„	16	20·79	„ 15
20·67	„	21	20·81	„ 9
20·67	„	4	21·03	„ 13

The middle value of these is 20·68; which will not be affected by omitting the first and last, as being doubtfully far from the proper value. The middle variation from the middle value is ·09; and as there are sixteen examples the probable error of the middle value will be this $\div \sqrt{15}$, which yields **20·68** inches ± ·03 for the mean cubit used at this place and period. The early cubit of 20·63 had therefore been lengthened to the value of 20·68 by the XVIIIth dynasty, and it lengthened slightly more on reaching Roman times.

CHAPTER IV.

THE MANUFACTURES.

51. The new capital of Akhenaten needed a large amount of decorative work, and suitable factories sprung up to supply the material. The glazes and glass were the two principal manufactures, and in those lines under the impulse of the new art a variety and a brilliancy was attained, which was never reached in earlier or later times. So far as the use of glazes is possible, this period shews the highest degree of success, and the greatest variety of application.

Fortunately the sites of three or four glass factories, and two large glazing works, were discovered; and though the actual work-rooms had almost vanished, the waste heaps were full of fragments which shewed the methods employed: moreover the waste heaps of the palace, as we have mentioned in Chap. II, contained hundreds of pieces of glass vases which illustrate the finished objects.

We can therefore now trace almost every stage and detail of the mode of manufacture; and in this chapter we shall follow the course of the processes employed for both glass and glazes.

52. We are already familiar with the frits made by the Egyptians, from the XIIth dynasty onward, for colouring purposes. These have been carefully analyzed and remade by Dr. Russell; and we know that the components were silica, lime, alkaline carbonates, and copper carbonate varying from 3 per cent. in delicate greenish blue, up to 20 per cent. in rich purple blue (see "Medum," p. 44). The green tints are always produced if iron be present; and it is difficult, if not impossible, to obtain silica from sand without the iron in it preventing the blues being produced.

One of the first requisites therefore is to obtain the elements of the mixture free from iron. How this could be done was quite unknown until I picked up a piece of a pan of frit, which had been broken in the furnace and rejected, before it was combined. This shewed clearly throughout the mass the chips of white silica; and from their forms they were clearly the result of crushing the quartz pebbles which are to be found on the surface of the desert, having been rolled down by the Nile from the disintegration of primitive rocks further south. The half-formed frit was of a fine violet colour, proving the freedom of it from iron. The lime, alkali, and copper had combined already, and the silica was in course of solution and combination with the alkali and lime, half dissolved like sugar stirred into a pudding. The carbonic acid in the lime and alkali had been partly liberated by the dissolved silica, and had raised the mass into a spongy paste. With longer continued heating the silica in ordinary samples has entirely disappeared, and formed a mixture of more or less fusible silicates. These made a pasty mass, when kept at the temperature required to produce the fine colours; and this mass was then moulded into pats, and toasted in the furnace until the desired tint was reached by the requisite time and heat; and a soft crystalline, porous, friable cake of colour was produced.

E

53. Among the furnace-waste were many pebbles of white quartz. These had been laid as a cobble floor in the furnace, and served as a clean space on which to toast the pats of colour, for scraps of the paste of frit were found sticking to one side of the pebbles. This floor also served to lay objects on for glazing, as the superfluous glaze had run down and spread over the pebbles as a thin wash of green. Doubtless this use of the pebbles was two-fold ; they provided a clean furnace floor, and they became disintegrated by the repeated heating so that they were the more readily crushed for mixture in the frits afterwards.

The half-pan of uncombined frit shews exactly the size and form of the fritting-pans, about 10 inches across and 3 inches deep. Among the furnace-waste were also many pieces of cylindrical jars, about 7 inches across and 5 inches high. These jars almost always had glaze run down the outside of them, from the closed end to the open end ; the glaze is of various colours, blue, green, white, black, etc., evidently leaked from the pans of glass. Hence they must have stood mouth downward in the furnace, to support the fritting-pans and glass crucibles above the fire, as shewn at the bottom of PL. XIII, 62.

54. Of the furnaces used for glass-making we have no example ; but a furnace that was found near the great mould and glaze factory was apparently used for charcoal-burning, as a great quantity of charcoal was found in it, but no trace of pans, jars, or glass. This furnace (see PL. XLII) was an irregular square varying from 43 to 57 inches at the sides. It was originally about 35 inches high, but the roof was destroyed. The northern door was 29 high and 15 wide, to admit the north wind, and to serve for tending the furnace on the windward side. While the south or exit door was 16 high and 13 wide, for the gases to pass off. Probably the glazing furnaces were on the same principle ; and perhaps even the same furnace would be used for varying purposes.

55. Of the stages of production of the glass we have a continuous series. The crucibles in which it was melted were deeper than the fritting-pans ; being about two or three inches in depth and diameter. The form is shewn by the outlines of the pieces of glass, and most fully by piece 40, PL. XIII, which gives a section of the vessel in which it cooled. Many such pieces of glass are found retaining the rough surface, and even chips of the crucible adhering to them ; while the old top surface shews the smooth melted face, with edges drawn up by capillary attrac-

tion. The upper part is often frothy and worthless. This proves that the materials were fused in these vessels, as the froth of carbonic acid expelled by combination was yet in the vessel. If the glass had been made eleswhere and then merely remelted here it would have been clear. Moreover, by the manner in which the crucible has in all cases been chipped off the lump of glass after cooling, it is certain that the glass was left to cool in the crucible ; so as to gradually let the scum rise, and the sediment sink, as is now done with optical glass. If the glass had been poured out, we should not have found such pieces as these ; on the contrary we ought then to have found masses of cast glass, which have never yet been discovered. It is therefore plain that the glass after melting was left to stand in the crucibles until the furnace was cool ; the blocks were then removed, the crucibles chipped away, the defective parts of the glass—scum and sediment—were chipped off, and a clear lump of good glass was thus obtained for working up.

While the glass was being made samples were taken out by means of a pair of pincers, to test the colour and quality ; and many of these samplings (as PL. XIII, 41, 42) were found, shewing the impress of the round-tipped pincers.

56. After obtaining the lumps of clear glass these were broken up into suitable sizes, and heated to softness. They were then laid on a flat surface, and rolled by a bar worked diagonally across them. This method prevents flattening in the roll, which is liable to occur in a pasty material if rolled at right angles to the length. Also a rolled paste is liable (like hammered iron rods) to become hollow in the middle owing to over expansion of the outside, and so to crack up lengthways. But by pressing only a short length at once in rolling, by a diagonal bar, the rest of the material holds it together and tends to prevent splitting. Again, by rolling only a small area at once, much greater pressure can be applied, and hence the glass could be rolled cooler, and without such risk of flattening. The marks of the diagonal rolling are seen on the finished rolls, as on PL. XIII, 43.

The next stages, after thus obtaining thick rods of glass, were to draw this out, as in producing what is now known as "cane" ; or to flatten it into strips, which were polished and used for inlaying, or else drawn out like the rods, thus forming thin glass ribbon. A third variety of drawn glass are the tubes, PL. XIII, 51, 52. How these were first made is uncertain, probably by heavy rolling of the rods, so as to make them hollow inside. These tubes were sometimes used for beads, and no other purpose for them has been noticed. In no case are they known to have been bent, to be formed into ornaments or syphons.

57. The usual mode of bead-making was by winding a thin thread of drawn-out glass around a wire, These wires are actually found with the beads still stuck on them (PL. XIII, 59–61). When I say wire, I do not mean necessarily drawn wire, as wire-drawing is not known till Roman times, if then. (The piece of wire rope in the Naples Museum needs some voucher for its age.) And what appears like bronze wire, that I have found of the XVIIIth dynasty shews facets of hammering when magnified.

Many beads were imperfectly formed, and left as spirals owing to the tail of glass thread not being united to the body of the bead. These are found of a corkscrew shape, as in PL. XIII, 53, etc. Some flat beads were made by coiling a long bead, flattening it, and then cutting it across, as in XIII, 57, 60. The pendant beads, up to 1¼ inches long, shew plainly the coils of the thread by which they were built up, in the clear structure of the glass. And every bead of this age shews more or less of the little peak at each end where the glass thread was finally separated from it. On the contrary the Coptic glass beads are all made by drawing out a glass tube, as shewn by longitudinal bubbly striations; and then the tube was rolled under an edge across it, to nick it, so as to break up into beads. It is impossible to confound a bead of the early process with one of the later.

The drawn-out glass rod was commonly used for bending into unclosed circles for ear-rings.

58. The most elaborate use of glass was for the variegated vases. These were all made neither by blowing nor by moulding in moulds, but by hand modelling. A tapering rod of metal was taken, as thick as the intended interior of the neck; on the end of this was formed a core of fine sand, as large as the intended interior of the vase. The rod and core were dipped in the melted glass and thus coated. The coat of glass was then hand-worked; the foot was pressed out into shape, like the pressed feet of the Roman glass cups; the brim was turned outward; the pattern was applied by winding thin threads of coloured glass around the mass, and rolling it so as to bed them into the body of the glass; the wavy design was made by dragging the surface upward or downward at intervals; the twisted margin of the brim, or the foot, was made by winding one thread of

glass spirally round another, and bending the two round the vase; the handles were attached; and as often as the glass became too cool to work in any of these processes, the end of the rod could be just placed into the furnace, and the half-formed vase warmed up to working point. When the whole was finished, the metal rod in cooling would contract loose from the glass; it could then be withdrawn, the sand core rubbed out, and the vase would be finished.

Of the fragments of vases of which enough remained to shew the design clearly, and which had a distinct pattern, the number of pieces was—

Single-dragged	160
Double-dragged	36
Twirled	36
Eyed	42
Spirals . . . . . , .	2
White blotches	3
Bowls	3

The single-dragged are those only dragged in one direction on the face, forming a pattern of UUUUU ; the double-dragged are those dragged alternately in each direction, forming a pattern of WWWW.

This style of glass descended into Greek times, and was largely used in Magna Graecia ; but the later styles are all coarser, and have not the brilliancy and flat face that mark these earlier products, which are now firmly dated to 1400 B.C.

59. Beside the working of glass in a soft state, there was also good work in cutting and engraving. There are pieces of glass with polished faces and cut mouldings ; with engraved patterns ; with engraved subjects (as various rings, etc., XIV, 23, 53 ; XV, 133); a piece of an opaque white glass bowl, imitating fine limestone, and deeply engraved for inlaying ; rich blue glass volutes for inlaying, probably in alabaster, like the blue glass and alabaster frieze of Tiryns ; and hieroglyphs for inlaying in the walls, cut in glass.

60. The colours are very varied, and in sorting over hundreds of the drawn glass rods it seemed as if no two pots of glass had been quite alike; so that a few pieces of each batch might be found, but no exact match beyond those. There are purple, opaque violet, blue, green, yellow, opaque red, brown, black, and white. Most of these were both transparent and opaque; and the variety of blues and greens is indefinite.

61. Glazing was a highly developed art at this period, and reached its greatest successes under Akhenaten. Whole statues of glaze, and walls

blazing with glazed tiles and hieroglyphs, shewed how the difficulties of size had been overcome.

The most complete instance of glazing architecturally that we can restore is in the columns of the painted pavement No. 1 of the harem, (Plan PL. XXXVI). No trace or chips of stone columns remained there ; but great quantities of green-glazed tiles, ribbed to imitate bundles of reeds, (such as are upon the stone columns) ; lotus flowers, and buds on a triangular red ground to fit between the flowers, so as to appear as a garland of lotus flowers and buds on a red background ; also lotus petals, and green or red pieces to fit between them, to appear as a white petal-wreath on green or red ground. The reed tiles have projections at the end to fit under a retaining band ; and such a band on the stone columns is coloured yellow, so that it was probably of bright bronze, or gilded, on the glazed columns.

62. Inlayed glaze was also used effectively on the great capitals with gilding between, as shewn on the restoration in PL. VI. On the walls glazed tiles were much used ; all along the west side of the great hall of columns fragments of green tiles with daisies and thistles, were found scattered. Probably therefore there were more than two hundred feet of this tile dado, with inlayed white daisies and violet thistles. From the number of pieces of tile with water pattern, lotus, fishes, and birds, it seems that tiled floors also existed in the palace.

The stone walls were inlayed with glazed figures of birds, and glazed hieroglyphs ; the latter were both small and large, some of the cartouche borders being 4 inches wide, and discs of the Aten 8 inches across.

63. Glazes were also much used on portable objects. In the palace we found many pieces of dishes in the form of half fish, half yellow melons, half green gourds, etc. These from their richness and position were most likely part of the royal table-service. Vases were decorated with inlayed patterns of different colours, and also with applied moulded figures of flowers, etc. A favourite and beautiful style was of incising and inlaying dark-blue patterns on light-blue grounds. In other cases pale green was inlayed in violet (XIII, 18), or green in dark violet (XIII, 28, 37).

64. But the most wide-spread and popular use of glaze was for covering moulded figures, made for most diverse uses. Finger-rings (XVI, 161–240), decorations to stitch on dress (57, 59, 260, 436), inlayed hieroglyphs (241–269), pendants (271 *et seq.*), serpent's heads for cornices (322–327), flowers for inlaying (430, 456–506), fruits for pendants, inlaying, and ceiling reliefs (441–455), and geometrical pieces for inlayed patterns (558–594). These plates (XIV–XX) are drawn as if from the moulded objects ; where the objects have been found they are indicated by the letters of the colours (v, violet ; bl, blue ; gn, green ; y, yellow ; gy, grey ; wt, white ; bk, black) ; where they are drawn only from the moulds they are marked with M. In plates XIV, XV, where the numbers are important historically, the number of examples of each individual mould are given ; *e.g.* of No. 50 there are 4 impressions of one mould, and one each of three others, all in blue glaze ; also 4 moulds of one engraving, 3 of another, and 1 of a third.

An example of these moulds is shewn at the end (XX, 595). They are rough pats of baked clay, with the mark of the palm of the hand on the back ; a die was pressed on the clay, and so made the mould. After baking they were used apparently by taking an impression on a lump of moulding-paste, and then slicing the relief figure thus produced from off the lump with a sharp knife. These moulded figures were then dried, dipped in powdered glass, and fired to glaze them. Different lots of beads, etc., not yet glazed, shew that the moulding-paste was a very fine sand ; so white that perhaps powdered quartz was used, where the best blue had to be maintained free from iron.

65. We will now refer in detail to the plates of moulds XIV–XX, at any points that are not self-evident. Moulds were used as early as Amenhotep III, both for plaques (8) and for rings (9–19). The four objects of Tahutmes III were doubtless brought to Tell el Amarna as well as those of Amenhotep III, as only one impression of each of these was found, and no moulds or sculptures earlier than Amenhotep IV are known there. The figures 1, 2, 3, 5, 6, 7, 21, are all scarabs of stone, glazed.

The violet glass handle from some small object has been engraved before Amen was abandoned ; and the name of the god has been ground out of the cartouche. Nos. 25–32 are engraved metal rings or impressions of rings. Scarabs of Akhenaten are scarce, only five (33–37) having been found in all the work. The other numbers (38–64) are all moulded.

Of the Aten many moulded plaques were found, but never any scarabs, and only one ring (of limestone, 76). The moulds most usual are No. 70 ; these Aten moulds are exactly of the fabric of others of Akhenaten (47) and the queen (82), and are found with these north of the temple, in some part of the town, from whence the Arabs brought them to me.

The rings of the queen (83–89), of Ankhs-en-pa-aten (90–1) and the earlier type of Ra-smenkh-ka-ser-khepru, with the title "beloved of Ra-nefer-khepru" or of Uan-ra, i.e. of Akhenaten (92–95), were nearly all found in the rubbish mounds of the palace; the later types (97–102) were found in the town. The rings 103–5 are of great value as shewing the true name of Akhenaten's successor. Lepsius in the Denkmaler gives it as Ra-se-aa-ka-nekht-khepru in the only tomb where it was found; but Prisse gives that as Ra-se-hek-ka-ser-khepru (Mon. Eg. page 3). This inscription in the tomb is now totally destroyed, in the smashings made a few years ago: so that it can never be studied. These rings shew that *ser* is certainly the true reading and not *nekht* (the bull added in *Livre des Rois*, is without any authority); but whether the third sign is *aa*, *menkh* or *mer* is not clear, but it is clearly not *hek*; the rings certainly suggest *mer* or rather *menkh*. As the tomb was defaced and hard to read at this part, it seems that these readings of the rings are the best authority we have. This cartouche is the forerunner of Horemheb's name Ra-ser-khepru; and it might almost be thought that this king was the same as Horemheb, were not this a personal name, and Horemheb's a throne name.

Under Tutankhamen there is the curious double reading ring Aten or Amen (118); strictly the Amen is superfluous, as the name is Aten-(or Ra)-khepru-neb. It is clear that the return to Amen worship took place under Tut-ankh-amen, who probably then adopted this name; and afterwards placed Amen prominently forward as on Nos. 119–121.

The scarabs in the lower part of PL. XV should be noticed as shewing the date of these styles, which is otherwise unknown. Some of them (152, 154) are probably rather earlier.

66. The ring bezils are sometimes formed of a solid hieroglyph, such as the broken *nefer* (170) the eye (176) and the fish (195). The small ring (177) has a curious figure of the queen holding one of the little princesses by the hand, a large lotus bouquet in front, and the Aten rays descending overhead. It is of the same peculiar green as the rings of Ankh-s-en-pa-aten, and was evidently made at the same time.

The cylinders are probably due to foreign influence. The style of 181 and 183 is hardly Egyptian, but they were made at Tell el Amarna, as 181 is a mould, and the colour of the others is characteristic. The calves galloping on 182 are like the design of the painted pavement: this cylinder is of open or pierced work. In 183 the junction of the mould has been made down

the tree, the central object of the group; the cylinder having been broken in two at the junction, only half remains.

No. 184 seems to shew the royal bull trampling on an enemy. The prevalence of the ibex type, 187–194, is strange, as the animal does not seem to have ever been very common in Egypt; perhaps it was a "lucky" sign to wear, as it is marked *nefer* on 193.

The palmetto type (197–210) is here clearly derived from the blowing lotus, as shewn on 197–8, where the inner parts of the flower are well figured, rising out of the turned-back petals.

Imitation jewellery was a favourite device, and when well done with bright glazes the effect is not bad. In 222–3 a triple ring bezil with three coloured stones is shewn; the hollows left by the mould in 223 being intended to be filled with red and blue glaze, as in 222. The other forms, 224–234, are to imitate a set stone; and the lines radiating in most of them (224, 227–30) are copied from the puckering of a gold foil setting, when closed in around a stone.

The moulds for annular rings (235–6), for rings to which a separate bezil was fixed (237, 239–40), and for rings moulded with a bezil to be afterward graved (238) are all very common.

67. The groups of hieroglyphs (241–251) are probably intended for amulets and pendants; but some are for inlaying, as 247, 254, 257, 258, 262, 267, 269. The pendants were usually made by attaching a bead at the top (and often also at the base) by means of a touch of glaze fused on.

The figures 271–274 are evidently intended for the youthful Akhenaten. The number of gods made here, Osiris 277–8, Shu 279, Hathor 280–1, Ra 282, Mut 283–4, Bes 285–91, and the divine animals Tahuti 294, Taurt 295–9, and Hapi coming out of a shrine 303, shew that the manufacture was not limited to the fanatically Aten-worshipping times, but probably continued during the reign of Tut-ankh-amen like the making of royal rings. No. 301 is the body of a lion, to which the head would be fitted on. 302 is apparently a dog, the paws being all in one with the head, to be afterwards trimmed into form.

The birds 310–313 are for inlaying. The large snake heads 322–3 were moulded and finished by hand; they were used to form cornices of uraei, and pieces of them are common. There are many sizes, some being larger than these. The frogs, 328–9, fish, scorpion, scarabs, and flies finish the list of animals.

68. We next have developments of vegetable forms, beads derived from seeds, palmetto and rosettes from

flowers. The number of divisions of the rosette is so irregular that I have stated it to each example, at the left hand corner ; such irregular numbers as 7, 11, 13, 14, 15, 17, 22, and 23 shew that the pattern was often done by mere repetition until the space was filled.

69. The fruits are grapes 441–448, dates 449–450 fig 451, grape and thistle 452, and pomegranates 453–5. The lotus flower is one of the commonest, especially used for architectural glazed ware decoration, with the triangular red piece (459) to go between the flowers, bearing a bud. Nos. 474–6 are in the round. But for personal ornament the thistle was more used (479–498) as it gave such a scope for green and violet combined. No. 500 was to have a centre of different colour inserted. Nos. 501–504 are calyxes in the round.

70. Buds (505–6) were made in the round. Petals were used for flat inlay (507–512) ; but the pieces 513–5 may be merely geometrical, 515 being for the last piece in the inlays on the ribs of columns (see PL. VI). Lotus petals were commonly made into garlands, and hence were imitated for garland decoration (516) with intermediate pieces to give a red or green ground between them (517). Petals were also used for pendants on necklaces (518–20), and leaves with a mid rib 525–7. The ribbed pieces appear to be for backgrounds between other flowers (531–7), but 538–9 may be for thistles. Compound pieces of petal and background were made together (540–1). There are also the trefoil (542–3), palm-branch (544–5), and an unknown leaf. The drop pendants (548–550), are very common, and may be merely geometrical. Stars and crescents are not very usual. The remainder are all geometrical pieces, mostly for inlaying in stone work ; but 576 is a hollow hemisphere for threading as a boss in patterns.

Such moulds have been found in many other places, Memphis, Thebes, Gurob, &c. : but none are before the middle of the XVIIIth dynasty, from which they descend to Roman times. The development of them at Tell el Amarna seems fuller than elsewhere ; only a few dozen being occasionally obtained in other places, whereas I brought nearly five thousand from Tell el Amarna, after rejecting large quantities of the commonest ; and these comprise over five hundred varieties here illustrated, beside many smaller differences. All of these I have classified into series, and many of the sets have been given to public museums ; other sets remain awaiting distribution to collections as opportunity may arise. Of the moulded objects about two thousand were found, including fragments.

71. The pottery found at Tell el Amarna is closely like what I have before published from Gurob. Scarcely any perfect jars were found, but large quantities of fragments of blue painted ware had been thrown into old sand-pits to fill them up at the time of building the town, and hence they are dated to the earlier years of Akhenaten. The blue paint (frit) is very finely ground, and very intense ; it is used with black and red (lampblack and burnt ochre), and the ground tint is a light warm brown. The patterns are usually lotus, grapes and vine leaves, and garlands. The oil jars found thrown away in the corner of the hall were painted coarsely around the shoulder with a garland, done in green, red, and white.

The basis of the pottery is usually rather coarse soft brown ware, often faced with a polished coat of red. Another kind which was much better was a thin hard ruddy brown paste, with white speckles throughout it ; this is usually faced with a drab-white polished facing, very smooth and fine—a style characteristic of the end of the XVIIIth dynasty.

A favourite decoration in this period was with heads of Hathor or of Bes in relief ; fragments of a great Hathor bowl were found in the tomb of Akhenaten (as Mr. Wilbour informs me), and other such decorations were in the town.

The wine jars were capped with large masses of mud, and sealed with a great variety of seals, which are shewn in PL. XXI.

72. The sculptors' workshops proved of much interest. The most extensive was at the north of the palace, where the funeral furniture for Akhenaten had been prepared, as already described. Fragments of statues, trial pieces of an arm, a foot, hieroglyphs with master's corrections in black ink, and pieces of various works in stone and glaze were found here. One piece of glazed green ware with parts of cartouches must have been of a large size, the cartouches alone being probably 10 inches high. Another sculptors' place was found near the south end of the town, containing many stages of work, from the first practice of the beginner on the simplest sign, the *neb* (XI, 4) to more advanced studies from life (XI, 2), and even highly finished trial pieces. The best trial piece is one of the finest pieces of work found, (I, 8, 9) with a head of Akhenaten on one side; and a horse's head on the other ; the latter is merely roughed out, but is more able than any other early figure of the horse. Another trial piece shews an aged queen wearing the uraeus, who at this place can be no other than Thyi ; and another female head (I, 6) is

clearly of the same person, by the likeness. The triad of Akhenaten, queen, and princess, (I, 1) is also a trial piece, perhaps a sketch for the design of some large group. And the head of Akhenaten (I, 5) is on a slab which does not appear to have come from any building, and is probably a trial. The sweeping destruction of the buildings in ancient times, and of the figures in the tombs in modern times, has left us almost dependent for portraiture on the trial pieces which were carefully wrought, and buried as waste before the times of destruction. Considerable attempts were made at plaster casting ; not only is there the cast of Akhenaten's head, but also many pieces of cartouches, &c., all from the W. end of the Temenos.

73. Of metal work little was found ; the materials were gold, electrum, hard alloy like speculum metal, bronze and lead. No silver, tin, or iron occurred ; the latter metal has never yet been found by me before the XXIIIrd dynasty, in all the large clearances of Kahun, Gurob, and Tell el Amarna. There is nothing peculiar in the metal working, the bronze being mainly for knives, kohl sticks, &c., like those of Gurob. In a previous visit I obtained a piece of an Osiris cast by the *cire perdue* method, which is only about $\frac{1}{50}$ of an inch thick, the finest casting I have seen. Also I then got a bronze needle with two eyes at right angles, enabling two coloured threads to be sewn at once.

74. The weights are not numerous, only twelve being found of Egyptian date, beside a small set of six leaden weights of Roman age.

The kat standard is but a quarter of the whole series.

		Present.	Ancient.	X	Standard.
PL. XIII.					
6	Bronze and lead. Bull's head.	1353·7	1352·	10	135·2
	Limestone ball inscribed " 10 utens."	13859·	13880·	100	138·8
4	Alabaster cylinder.	729·1	729·6	5	145·9

Another bull's head of similar form, but smaller, was found at Gurob, and has remained unpublished, as I did not recognise it as a weight ; it is

		Present.	Ancient.	X	Standard.
	Bronze and lead. Bull's head.	304·9	307	2	153·5

The gold weight of 200 grains—or Aeginetan—is the commonest, over half the number being on that standard.

		Present.	Ancient.	X	Standard.
1	Red limestone, disc.	790·6	790·6	4	192·7
7	Alabaster, ovoid.	397·7	397·8	2	198·9
5	Alabaster, cone.	397·9	398·2	2	199·1
2	Alabaster, ovoid.	599·9	601·4	3	200·5
	Red sandstone, rough like 11.	1227·5	1232·	6	205·3
9	White limestone, disc.	52·5	52·6	¼	210·4
10	Alabaster, ovoid.	630·9	639·	3	213·

The last example may be an Assyrian weight of 5 shekels of 127·8 : another may be also Assyrian, but it is doubtful if it has not lost a great part since it was made.

		Present.	Ancient.	X	Standard.
	Gray granite, domed type.	39017	?	300	130·0

Of the Phœnician there are two examples.

		Present.	Ancient.	X	Standard.
11	White limestone, oblong.	1107·2	1107·5	5	221·5
9	Bronze, domed type.	235·0	235	1	235·
	(?) Grey granite (above). ?	39017	47000 (?)	200	235·

The leaden weights of Roman age are about the Constantine period, by the style of a glass spindle whorl found with them. They are on the basis of the stater or half shekel of the Ptolemaic system derived from the Phoenician.

		Present.	Ancient.	X	Standard.
	Flat domed type. 111111 111111	1379·3	1377	12	114·7
	Cube. 111 111	696·2	694	6	115·7
	Cube. 111 11	566·6	564	5	112·8
	Cube. 111	348·4	347	3	115·7
	Cube. 11	225·0	226	2	113·0
	Cube. 1	191·0	190	?	190

It is remarkable that the Assyrian is almost unknown among these weights, considering the relations of Akhenaten with Mesopotamia. At Gurob, in the same period, the order of frequency is Kat, Assyrian, Attic, Aeginetan, Phoenician ; a very different frequency to that of Tell el Amarna, where the Aeginetan is the commonest.

CHAPTER V.

THE JAR INSCRIPTIONS.

By F. LL. GRIFFITH.

75. The jars, of which Mr. Petrie brought back so large a number of the inscribed fragments, held a variety of liquids and solids, wine, oil, honey, preserved meat, etc. Most of the inscriptions contained dates of the reigning kings: and although the king's name is never stated, it is possible to supply the omission with considerable certainty, and therefrom to draw valuable historical inferences. (See PLS. XXII to XXV.)

The whole series may be tabulated thus:—

Year.	Wine.	Oil.	Meat.	*Shedh.*	Honey.	Fat.	*Bak.*
Reign of Akhenaten's successor, Rasmenkh-ka.							
1	0						
2	3	25					
3	..	1	..	..	..	2	
Reign of Amenhotep IV.							
4	3						
5	8						
Amenhotep IV. under the name Akhenaten.							
6	6						
7	8		..	1			
8	11		..	1	..	..	1
9	5		..	2			
10	3		..	3	1		
11	8		..	1	1		
12	5		..	1	1		
13	3						
14	7		..	..	..	1	
15	2		..	..	..	1	
16	9						
17	6						
18	0						

The wine series, being the most complete, is the first to engage our attention. The numbers for the 10th, 13th, and 15th years happen to fall very low for some reason that is probably no longer discoverable; perhaps the wine of those years was scanty or bad of quality, or the jars may have been thrown away in places which the Arabs have not yet plundered.

But the most remarkable feature is the absence of the first and third years, leaving the second isolated. When it is remembered that the building of Tell el Amarna was begun in the 6th year of Akhenaten, it becomes clear that this is no accident.

The dates of the reign of Amenhotep IV., afterwards called Akhenaten, evidently begin with the three examples of wine of the 4th year—already perhaps two years old when Amenhotep IV. commenced the building of his new capital—and thence continue steadily to what must be the end of Akhenaten's reign in his 17th year. The few dates previously known reached only to the 12th year.

The date of the year 2 must then belong to a different reign: as the series should be continuous, we must endeavour to explain how the three specimens of the year 2 can have been written in the year following the six specimens of the year 17. This can be accounted for plausibly in either of two ways. Akhenaten may have associated his successor on the throne with himself for a year before his death, so that the year 2, the first of his successor's sole reign, would follow immediately on his own 17th year—or, Akhenaten may have died towards the end of one year, after the vintage had taken place, so that there was no wine bottled in the four months which remained for his successor's first year. But this is unlikely, as the regnal years appear to have started from the day of accession. A single sherd appeared to have a date of the year 1, but as the numeral was indistinct and might possibly have been either 5 or 10 it could not be accepted as evidence.

Akhenaten was followed on the throne by his son-in-law, Ra-smenkh-ka-ser-kheperu: it is to him therefore that we must attribute the date of the year 2 on the wine potsherds. At the same time oil, of which there is no trace previously, was in great demand here. No less than twenty-five jars of the second year and one of the third are represented in the collection, as well as two jars of fat of the third year after the storage of wine there had ceased. These dates are the only evidence that we have of the duration of Ra-smenkh-ka's reign.

Such, I venture to think, is the most valuable part of the information to be obtained from the potsherds. Their fragmentary condition, and the indistinctness of the writing, rob us of much that would probably be of considerable value.

76. The wine series extending from the fourth year of Akhenaten to the second of Smenkh-ka-ra, consists of a very large number of extremely fragmentary specimens: a complete inscription (No. 28) runs—

> Year 7
> Wine good good (*i.e.*, very good) of the house of Aten
> The inspector Tu.

Another (No. 27)—

> Year 9
> Wine of the house of Aten
> Brought by the inspector Ab?

The ordinary formula (see Nos. 16, 23, etc.), always imperfect, is—

Year : . . . .
Wine of the house of Aten
West river · chief of the vineyard N.

On a few the names of the chiefs of the vineyard are faintly visible, and may be read, Seta(s) 89, 92), Ani (23, 2nd) ; Pa-aten-hes-su (24), the word *hes* is clear on one example, Hui-nefer (26), Hatta (29), Hui (30), Khai (94), Nefer-hotep (96), Zai (97). The "western river" is very frequent. We have also (15) the "western river in (?) the southern *bah* of the castle." In all probability the western river is identical with the Bahr Yusuf. Memphis is mentioned on 93, and the "northern oasis" (*i.e.*, El Khargeh) on 94.

Besides the "house of Aten" we find often "the house of Ankh-aten" (29, 30), and once "[the house of] Aten? in Memphis" (31). Also once (13) "the house of the sun rejoicing in the horizon (Akhet)." This is a title of the Aten deity, and is important as giving the man with raised arms as a variant of the hieroglyphics—hāï. A dated potsherd of the fourth year (91) is interesting for its reference to the "house of Ra Harakhti" (Ra, Horus of the two horizons), in place of the "house of Aten." Ra Harakhti was really the deity of the Aten worship. During the earliest stage of the heresy, at Thebes, the hawk-headed human form was actually retained in representations, but afterwards, at Akhetaten (Tell el Amarna), it was replaced by the many-armed disk or Aten. The inscription just quoted in fact shews us Amenhotep IV. as a worshipper of the Ra-Harakhti, a year or two before the Aten-worship was adopted.

We also find the "house of Ra who is in *Kebhu* (at Heliopolis ?)" (76), and "the house of Neith in . . . ." (85). The reference to Neith is remarkable ; probably these also date from before the establishment of the Aten-worship.

Other sherds introduce the names of kings, "[the house of Amen]hotep neter hak uas" (*i.e.*, Amenhotep IV. before he changed his name) (12), "the house of Akhenaten of long life" (8, 88) ; "the house of the queen" (11, 90) ; and "the house of Thyi" (14). "The house of Neb maat ra" (Amenhotep III.) (4 and 3) ; and "[the house of] Kha-em-maat" (the same) (9). There are several of "the house of Sehotep-ra" (5) ; "of Sehotep-aten" (21), perhaps heretical designations of Amenhotep III., avoiding the hated name of Amen. No. 10 gives the

temple (?) of Ra-aa-kheper-ka (Thothmes I.). One sherd mentions "wine of the house of the great seer," *i.e.*, the chief priest of the sun (6) ; another (3), more perfect, runs—

"Year 16 wine good good of the tribute of [the house of ?]
the great seer of the Aten Ra-mery."

The tomb of this highly-honoured priest at Tell el Amarna is well known.

77. The other classes may be dismissed in a few words.

Oil, *neheh*, is found on numerous sherds, of which all the examples, except one, date from the second year, and they are in better condition than any of the other series. No. 32 reads—

"Year 2 oil of the house of Aten brought by the *her pedt* chief of the mercenaries (or of transport ?) Ra, son of Ra-mai, purified by the superintendent of ointment Ray son of Ramai and the guardian Apy."

In one case the first officer is named Hui, and the second Aniy (No. 36).

But the oil was often brought by a *her menshu* or chief of trading-ships ? Unfortunately their names are not clearly legible. The officers charged with clarifying are the same as before (Nos. 38–42).

Next in importance is the

Meat, *auf der*, perhaps "pounded meat," or at least meat preserved in some way. In the Theban tombs we see wild-fowl plucked and stowed in jars, no doubt with salt ; perhaps the meat preserved in these jars at Tell el Amarna was of a similar kind. *Auf der* is amongst the provisions named in a papyrus of the time of Amenhotep III. (Mariette, Papyrus de Boulaq, Tome II, PL. III). The sherd No. 101 appears to be a fragment of a list of various meats.

The dates extend from the seventh to the twelfth year.

No. 46. "Year 10 preserved meat of the festival of Aten . . . Ankh-aten of the *Akhit* of Pharaoh."

Akhit is a new word, meaning perhaps "kitchen." It is evidently a name chosen for its alliteration with Akhenaten, Akhetaten, etc.

In one case (43) meat has been potted in the year 10 in a jar that had held wine of the year 5.

On some of these meat jars "children of the Aten" are mentioned (44–5, 98) ; and 54, 87 give—

"Year 7 preserved meat (?) . . . storehouse of (or for) the Ka of Ankh-ra (life of Ra) . . . feast of Ankh-aten."

Shedeh dates from the year 10 to the year 12. It

F

appears to be supplied by a gardener, like the wine.

"[Shed]h of eating, good good" is on one (65).

Honey dates from the years 14 and 15. A fragment shews a curious symbol of a man tying a bundle (62).

Fat (year 3) was "prepared in the Akhit" like the meat (72–3).

Bak "olive oil" (year 8) is specified as "sweet" and "best" (67–8).

Seremt (no date) is found several times (69) ; on (97) it is qualified as "good seremt of the queen." The equivalent word in Coptic means "wine lees."

"*Nehimaa* twice excellent" is found once (80).

The "white house" (81), and "white house of Pharaoh" (82), "the scribe Rui" (84), "the scribe Besi" (86), are the legends on several single specimens· One longer inscription (77), unfortunately not decipherable, mentions the country of Airsa, the Alashiya of the cuneiform despatches, and terminates with "12 ? *henu*" or "pints" as the amount of the contents.

Several fragments of blue painted ware, of a different class from the rest, had portions of a legend referring to the "eye-ball," and may possibly have been connected with eye-salve (74–5).

The last four specimens on PL. XXIV, marked 87 to 90, are selected from a small series obtained from the Arabs in 1892 by Mr. Percy Newberry, and kindly lent by him for comparison. They are of value especially as helping to complete the legends on some of the others. In 1893 Mr. Howard Carter purchased a larger number, resulting in the addition of PL. XXV, and of several to the table of dates.

CHAPTER VI.

THE CUNEIFORM TABLETS.

By Prof. A. H. SAYCE, D.D.

78. The cuneiform tablets found by Prof. Petrie at Tel el-Amarna have an importance far beyond what their fragmentary condition might lead us to expect. On the one hand they have determined the exact spot in which the foreign correspondence of Khu-n-Aten was carried on, and have shewn that the *fellahin* gave me correct information when they shewed me, four years ago, the place where the tablets had been discovered ; on the other hand they have proved that the Babylonian scribe, or scribes, of the Egyptian Pharaohs worked with the help of dictionaries and lists of characters, and that lexicons had been compiled for their use. The beginnings of a comparative study of languages can thus be traced back to the age of the Eighteenth Dynasty.

Only one of the fragments was found in a room of what we may call the Egyptian Foreign Office. It is that which is numbered XI in the accompanying Plate XXXII, and, characteristically enough, is a portion of a dictionary of Semitic Babylonian and Accado-Sumerian. All the other fragments were lying in rubbish-holes above which the Foreign Office was built. As there are among them letters from Rib-Hadad the governor of Gebal and other Egyptian officials, it is clear that the Office in question must have been built after the foreign correspondence of the Pharaohs had been removed from Thebes to the new capital of Khu-n-Aten, and probably also after the receipt of a certain amount of correspondence in the new capital itself. The fragments therefore must all be earlier than the closing years of Khu-n-Aten's reign.

79. The largest of the fragments· (No. 1 of the Plate XXXI) is shewn by the forms of the characters employed in it to have probably been sent from the land of the Amurrâ or Amorites. This was the country which lay immediately to the north of the later Palestine, and in which was situated Kadesh on the Orontes, the southern capital of the Hittites in the following century. Reference is twice made in the fragment (lines 2 and 5) to a certain El-ebed (written Il-abta in line 5), who is otherwise unknown. The name may also be read Il-ardata, like that of Suyardata one of the Palestinian governors. *Arda* in Babylonian corresponded to Abdu (Heb. *ebed*) in Canaanitish. The formation of the name is very strange, since it ought to be Ebed-el "servant of God," instead of the converse El-ebed. Perhaps it is a literal translation of a construction of the Amorite language, which may have placed the governing noun before the governed, contrary to the usage of the Semitic tongues. In the first paragraph of the letter it is said that "he has taken him in (the city ?)," but the captive cannot have been El-ebed, since immediately afterwards we read of "El-ebed along with him." The last line of the paragraph states that "[he lifted up] the hands before the gods."

The next paragraph begins with the assertion that "thou knowest that his father did" (*ippus*) something the account of which is lost. Then the writer goes on to declare that "I defend them," and that "the officer possesses" something derived from "his father." There is nothing in any of the Tel el-Amarna correspondence otherwise known which throws any light on all this.

Two more fragments (Nos. 2 and 3 Pl. XXXI) belong to letters from Rib-Hadad the governor of northern Phœnicia, the seat of whose government was at Gebal. Mention is made in them of the city of Tsumuri, the Zemar of Gen. x. 18, the Simyra of classical geography, now Sumra. Zemar was the most important of the inland fortresses which were under Rib-Hadad's charge, and the loss of it in the closing years of the reign of Khu-n-Aten was one of the signs of the overthrow of the Egyptian empire in Asia. Mention is further made of " Ebed-Asirte (or Ebed-Asherah) [thy] servant," who subsequently became a bitter enemy of Rib-Hadad, and a rebel against the authority of the Pharaoh. He and his sons overran the land of the Amorites, and it was to them that the fall of Zemar was due.

In fragment No. 2 (line 3) Rib-Hadad calls himself—as elsewhere in his letters—"the appointed" or "legitimate servant" of the Egyptian king (*arad kiti*). He also speaks of "the city of Tisa . . .," otherwise unknown, which he describes as in the "district of Zemar." In fragment 3 (line 4) reference is made to "the country of the Amorites," which is called by its Sumerian name of Martu, and the Pharaoh receives his usual titles of "the king, the sun-god, my lord." The last line of the fragment contains the words: "the house of the king my lord."

Fragment No. 4 begins with the words: "the country of the king," and a city is mentioned which is described as "a garrison." But beyond this fact, and the further fact that the writer speaks of his "chariots," the broken character of the text does not allow us to obtain any information from it.

80. In fragment No. 5 we have a specimen of one of the dictionaries to which I have already alluded. What is left of it makes us regret that there is not more. From the colophon on the reverse we gather that the dictionary was compiled under the direction of the Egyptian king, what remains of the first line reading [*ki*] *pi sar mat Mitsri* "by order of the king of Egypt." Of the rest of the colophon I can translate only the 4th and 6th lines; "foods and 7 fruits (?) of the countries"; "from the clerks."

The obverse, however, is more intelligible. In the first column are the Semitic equivalents of an ideograph, the Sumerian pronunciation of which is given in the second column. The arrangement of the dictionary thus differs from that of the dictionaries which were compiled in Babylonia and Assyria, where the ideographs are placed in the second column and the Semitic equivalents in the third. The reason of such a different arrangement is clear. In Babylonia the standard literature and literary language of the country were Sumerian; it was consequently the Sumerian words which had to be explained and translated into Semitic. Hence they occupied the first place in the lexical works. In Egypt, on the other hand, the Semitic Babylonian was the standard language, a knowledge of Sumerian being of little importance except in so far as it enabled the scribe to understand the ideographs of the cuneiform script. In the dictionaries of Tel el-Amarna, therefore, Semitic Babylonian has the place of honour, while the Sumerian words are relegated to the second column.

That the words belong to the Sumerian language we know from the fact that the Babylonian *da-du* "a darling" is given in the fragment as the equivalent of *ki-im* or *kim*, and one of the Assyrian lexical tablets (W. A. I. v. 16. 34.) informs us that *kim* was the Sumerian word for *dâdu*. So, too, *muru* "a youngling" is the rendering of *tur-tur*, and *tur-tur* signified "little" in the præ-Semitic language of Chaldæa.

But the dictionary contains philological information with which we were not previously acquainted. We learn from it that *dadu* was not only the equivalent of the Sumerian *kim*, but also of a word *til*. To what language *til* may have belonged we do not know. It may have belonged to Sumerian, but if so it is a new addition to our stock of Sumerian words. *Milkutu* "a kingdom" and [*e*]*bisu* "a performer" are further given as translations of *tur-tur*. This, too, is new, and it is possible that the translations may throw light on the name of the king of Goyyim who was the ally of Chedor-laomer in his war in Palestine (Gen. xiv. 1). His name is written Thorgal in the Septuagint, and since *gal* in Sumerian and *khali* in Kassite signified "great" it may be that in Thorgal we have to see a Tur-gal or "great prince."

The second ideograph in the fragment is represented in the Sumerian column by the word *aga*. This, in fact, as we already knew, is its Sumerian value. But what the Semitic words may be by which *aga* is rendered, I have no idea. Only their terminations remain, and these terminations do not suit any of the known Semitic equivalents of *aga*. This may also be the case as regards the Semitic equivalents of the ideograph which follows if they are to be read *da-sum-mu* and [*da-*]*sa-mu*. But since the ideograph is rendered by the Semitic *simtu* "destiny" in the Assyrian texts, it is possible that we should make *sum-mu* and *sa-mu* independent words, *samu* being a common Assyrian verb meaning to "appoint," from which *simtu* is derived. The value *khis* is assigned to the ideograph itself. This is new, since in the lexical tablets of Nineveh the value attached to it is that of *khas* and not *khis*. The ideograph preceding *aga*, to which the value of *kur* is attached, may be the same as that which in W. A. I. ii. 47. 3. forms the name of a deity, since *kur* is given as its pronunciation, though in the published copy its form is the same as that of the ideograph *khas*, *khis*.

Fragment No IV is again a portion of a dictionary, but a dictionary of a different nature from that which we have just been considering. Here in the first column Semitic words and ideographs are grouped together as translations of Sumerian words which are phonetically spelled out. The Semitic *risapu* and [*di*]*kate* are given along with the ideographs [G A Z]-G A Z as the equivalents of the Sumerian *ga-az-ga-az* "slaughter." Small as it is, this fragment is of importance, as it tends to shew that Sumerian was still a spoken language in the age of the Eighteenth Egyptian dynasty. Otherwise it is difficult to understand why such pains should have been taken to compile a list of Sumerian words, and to indicate their exact pronunciation, for the use of Egyptian scribes who when they wrote in cuneiform ordinarily employed the language of Semitic Babylonia. If they never had occasion to make use of Sumerian, they would not have undertaken a work which even the *literati* of Babylonia and Assyria considered superfluous.

Fragments VII, VIII, and X belong to letters; beyond this it is impossible to say anything about them. Fragment VII begins with a man's name, the first syllable of which is *Ar*, and in fragment VIII the word "silver" is thrice mentioned.

The clay cylinder (No. IX) is interesting, as it is an imitation in clay of the stone cylinders which the Babylonians wore attached by strings to their wrists, and which they used as seals. The inscription upon it reads *Dupsar Te-tu-nu na sa Samsu-ni-ki*, which I should translate "the seal of Tetunu the man of Samas-niki." The last name, however, may perhaps be read Samas-akhi-iddina. In any case it is a Babylonian name, while Tetunu seems to be Egyptian. In Samas-niki or Samas-akhi-iddina we probably have the name of the official who conducted the correspondence of the Egyptian Foreign Office, Tetunu being his clerk. Whether this be so or not the name is an evidence of the influence exercised by Asiatics at the court of Khu-n-Aten, where one of the members of the Foreign Office traced his descent from the distant land of Babylonia.

Fragment XI is part of another "dictionary," but the explanation of it is difficult. On the obverse we twice have the word *nun-zu* "he does not know," and on the reverse the third column contains the characters *ya-an*, that is *yan*, while in the second column we find *a-av-ni* and *a-ya-na*, the Semitic Babylonian equivalents of these words being apparently given in the fourth column. To what language the words *yan*, *âvni* and *ayana* may belong I cannot say, but they are not Semitic.

Fragment XII is a list of cuneiform characters arranged according to the appearance of their Babylonian forms. Among them are the characters *elim*, *uk*, *kis* (?), *qar*, *dar*, *sul*, and *tsu*. In fragments XIII and XIV we have a table of ideographs with their significations in Semitic, the ideograph for "gate," for example, being represented by the Semitic *babu*. What Fragment XV may have been it is not easy to say, since it contains an Egyptian proper name Riya-ba.., the first element of which represents the name of the Egyptian Sun-god. Fragment XVI comes from a letter and mentions "the god Merodach." Fragment XVIII also comes from a letter, but all that is distinguishable upon it with certainty are the words "city" and "house." Fragment XVII seems to be the exercise of some scribe who used the forms of the cuneiform characters employed by the Amorites and repeated in them the proper name Galas-du... The name appears to be Amorite as well as the forms of the characters, so that the scribe was probably an Amorite by birth.

The last Fragment (XVIII *bis*) is the commencement of a letter from [Sutar]na the governor of the city of Musikhuni. Another letter of his exists which is now at Berlin (Winckler and Abel: *Mittheilungen aus der orientalischen Sammlungen*, III, No. 130), and it is from this that we know how to supply the first two syllables of Sutarna's name. Musikhuni is probably the city of Masakh mentioned by Thothmes III at Karnak among the towns of northern Palestine. Mr. Tomkins identifies it with Meskhah 3½ miles south-west of Sarona.

My copies of Prof. Petrie's tablets were made at Tel el-Amarna, or rather Haggi Qandîl, shortly after their discovery. Mr. Strong copied them independently after their arrival in England, and has been good enough to enumerate the places in which our copies differ. Apart from corrections which have been introduced in this description, he notes that in No. I, line 1, he sees the traces of *ẓ* (?) after the last character *num*; in line 6, he reads, instead of the first character, the Amorite form of *us*, and *du* instead of the fifth; and in line 9 the third character is *us*. In No. IV, line 4, he makes the last two characters *us-al* (?) instead of my *pu-nu*.

CHAPTER VII.

FLINT TOOLS FROM TELL EL AMARNA.

By F. C. J. SPURRELL, F.G.S.

81. These implements and waste flakes were found in two localities; the sickle flints in presumably a workshop near the palace waste heaps, the rude flakes in a large heap in the south end of the town. The quality of the flint calls for no particular notice, but some thin flat pieces were parts of river-worn pebbles, which, having lain on the surface, had been split by the action of the weather, aided by blowing sand. These were doubtless collected with a view to use, as was found to have been the case in some of Mr. Petrie's discoveries of the same date at Gurob. The artificial flakes consist of flat thin ones, and others of straight prismatic form. In both cases they were struck on the spot from the block, as is seen by the close resemblance of the texture, blots, and stains in them. Of the thin flat varieties some closely resemble in form and size the leaf-shaped ones met with at Gurob (see "Illahun" by W. M. F. Petrie, pl. XVI). Altogether the irregularity of the flaking and chipping is very apparent, shewing uncertainty in the operator.

No knives or large tools were found. Of those whose form leaves us in no doubt as to their use, are sickle teeth in various states of manufacture; from those merely squared out of thin flakes, to those which had been mounted in a sickle and still have the cement adhering to them. The completed teeth comprise all the various forms required by the different parts of the implement, but the neatness of form and correct adaptation to the groove for which they were intended is wanting, as compared with those of early date from Kahun. The denticulations on these teeth are of three sorts. Some are fairly good and regular, but inferior to the best XIIth dynasty examples; moreover these are the only ones having signs of usage, thus suggesting that they are old ones of an earlier date re-employed. The next are denticulated, but of an almost wild irregularity of manufacture, altogether suggestive of trial pieces; bad

as they are, however, the adherent cement shews them to have been set. None of these have any wear or polish; and one tooth which had been set is smooth at the edge, and no denticulation has been even attempted. Another large one, with the cement adhering completely, consists of a knife-blade of good work, and perhaps of early date, which had been broken at the ends until about 3½ inches long. It has no further adaptation to its newer use in the way of denticulation, and it is very blunt. The third kind appears to be mere spalls on which the chipping of the denticulations was tried and practised by ignorant or idle people. This trial was rather freely carried on. Ill made or irregular flakes having been taken, some were roughly indented on all sides without any meaning, while others curiously simulate ragged arrow-heads. But as these are ill suited for such a purpose, and as they may be seen to connect themselves by gentle gradations with others shaped like a boot, a kite, or other accidental oddity, they cannot be considered intentional efforts at arrow, or spear-head making. The mode in which all this denticulation was managed is clear, and the worn edges of some of the flakes shew that they were the tools employed. Thus, the flake to be nicked was held horizontally, and a large flat thin-edged one was used to strike the side of that perpendicularly, and so to notch it. We have then a state of workmanship such as any of us may repeat off-hand with the spare flakes from the collection, and so obtain precisely similar results.

82. The teeth have in many cases the cement with which they were fastened to the sickle still adhering to them, as seen by the impressions of the grooves in which they were laid, yet left in the cement. Mostly these grooves were very slight, having wider angles than those of Kahun, while in a few cases there were no grooves at all, only a flat surface to which the tooth was attached in an upright position by the cement alone, and that position sometimes awry.

The cement is of various colours; mere brownish clayey sand, slate-grey clay, and sand with a green admixture. The cement is sometimes green throughout, sometimes the green is only a surface layer. It is never painted. The colour is sometimes merely of a faint green-grey shade, in others a fairly bright green. The medium in all cases is bees-wax. Water has no effect on the compound; all the specimens are hard when cold, but crush up when warmed to about the temperature of melting wax, and harden again on cooling. The fumes smell of wax and the compound bnrns with a clear flame. The wax may be wholly dissolved out by boiling alcohol and ether, and by chloroform, leaving mineral matter only. The proportions of wax employed vary. In a poor specimen, easily crumbled with the nail, I obtained 15 per cent. of wax. Others contain much more, and present a waxy lustre in a clean fracture, &c.

The colour is obtained by the use of different powdered minerals. Those actually found in use were a *felsite*, stained naturally with a copper infiltration ; and a sand consolidated with copper carbonate. These are natural. Other green minerals were collected ready for use. No artificial frit was found mixed with the wax.

The whole find suggests a workshop in which "properties" for state and religious shows were made by hasty or unskilled workmen. The woodwork was probably painted green, and the cement coloured to match it. The colouring of the sickles recalls the representation of the earliest hieroglyphs, and suggests symbolism rather than utility.

Of the remaining tools only a few pieces need be mentioned, which might have been used to scrape a limestone surface.

CHAPTER VIII.

HISTORICAL RESULTS.

83. In the history of the new departure of art, religion, and ethics at Tell el Amarna, the first question is the period of its rise. On no monument yet known is there any trace of the worship of the Aten in this peculiar style, until after the reign of Amenhotep III. Among the most prominent features of the new departure are the absence of the worship of any god except the Aten or sun, the representation of the sun with rays ending in hands which accept offerings and give the sign of life, and the great breadth of the cartouche band. The style of art is also distinctive, but less readily defined. As there is no trace of these peculiarities until after the death of Amenhotep III, so also there is no trace of any work at Tell el Amarna before that of the new style.

Probably the earliest monument of the new style is the cartouche of queen Thyi (PL. XLII) in the limestone quarry H, which is distinguished by the breadth of the cartouche band. Being alone, without any king's name, it appears as if she were sole regent : this would therefore be after the death of Amen-

hotep III, her husband, and before the active reign of Amenhotep IV, her son, during the first year or two after his accession.

84. But before considering his age, it will be best to deal with the question of his personality, and the identity of Amenhotep IV and Akhenaten. Strictly speaking it is impossible to prove that any past ruler has not obscurely died during his nominal reign, and been succeeded by another ruler who has adopted his names and titles, imitated all his peculiarities, and borne a close resemblance to him in face. Such may be the case with even any well-known king, as Ramessu II or Constantine, and such has even been reported of Napoleon III. But no such tale can be worth a thought unless some substantial reason can be alleged for the changeling hypothesis. It has been proposed that Amenhotep IV died after a very few years ; and that Akhenaten, a man, or a woman, was raised by intrigue into his vacant place, adopted his throne name, and his diadem name, and introduced the new style. It has been proposed that the new ruler was a woman, masquerading with a wife and suppositious children ; such a notion resting on the effeminate plumpness of Akhenaten, and the alleged prevalence of feminine courtiers. It has also been proposed that he was an eunuch.

We will now review the actual remains and see what they tell us.

85. Amenhotep IV is only represented as being married upon two monuments, namely, the blocks published by Prisse (Mon. Eg. XI, 3), and the piece of alabaster cup here published (PL. XIII, 23). In both cases his wife is Nefertythi, the same as the wife of Akhenaten. On the steles of Akhenaten dated in his sixth year there are sometimes one daughter, sometimes two ; where there is only one, a second and sometimes a third has been added later ; on the steles of the eighth year there are always two daughters. Hence we may conclude that his second daughter was born at the close of the sixth year of his reign ; and that he was probably married about the beginning of the fourth year of his reign. He therefore began his reign presumably as a child of about twelve years old ; for, as being the king, he would have been married early to avoid dynastic difficulties, and fifteen or sixteen would not therefore be an unlikely age for his marriage. We see then that Akhenaten began his reign as a minor under the tutelage of queen Thyi ; that Amenhotep IV is shewn as unmarried (Villiers Stuart's tomb) as well as married, and that his wife

had the same name as that of Akhenaten. There is no difficulty therefore in this point.

86. The portraiture has been supposed to be the most clear proof that Amenhotep IV and Akhenaten are different persons. On the facade of Villiers Stuart's tomb, the two are represented in a very different manner, and with great difference of features, But the face of Amenhotep IV is clearly that of a boy, and bears much resemblance to that of his father Amenhotep III. Can this boy Amenhotep be the same as the man Akhenaten ? Now Prisse publishes from Karnak (Mon. Eg. X, 1) a slab with Akhenaten adoring the Aten, but with undoubtedly the face of Amenhotep IV as on the Villiers Stuart tomb. How such a change is possible depends on his age. Children are often observed to resemble one parent, and yet to grow up more like the other. To suppose that Akhenaten was like his father when a boy, and that the likeness was exaggerated as being the fashionable face—yet that as his mind and body took shape between twelve and sixteen, under the vigorous and determined tutelage of his imperious mother Thyi, he should have grown into a nearer resemblance to her (PL. I, 6), seems not at all an unlikely state of the case. Moreover, the cast of his head (PL. I, 10) is of an expression betwixt that of the two portraits I, 7, 9, and links them together. We must remember that when once a standard portrait was adopted the artists would continue to copy it, and pupils would work on it in trial pieces, until some fresh type was promulgated. The chronology of the reign is also accordant. The latest date of Amenhotep IV is the fifth year (Gurob papyrus) and the earliest date of Akhenaten is the sixth year.

87. The question of identity may then be summed up thus. Amenhotep IV and Akhenaten both worshipped the Aten alike, they both had a wife of the same name, (Prisse, XI, 3, and cup), they both had two daughters (Prisse, XI, 3), they both had the same features (Prisse, X, 1), they both had the same throne name, they both specially honoured Māat or truth (Villiers Stuart's tomb, and the motto "*Ankh-m-maat*") and the reign of one ends in the fifth while the other begins in the sixth year. If such points are not sufficient to satisfy any one, it would be difficult to prove the continuity of the history of any king.

There is, however, yet the theory that Akhenaten was a woman, or an eunuch. As the body has not been recovered from the tomb, it is impossible to prove the case anatomically ; but on considering his

actions, how do such hypotheses appear ? Is it credible that the most uxorious king of Egypt, who appears with his wife on every monument, who rides side by side with her in a chariot, and kisses her in public, (tomb of Mahu), who dances her on his knee (PL. I, 16), who has a steadily increasing family—that this king was either a woman in masquerade or an eunuch ? Further, see the essential differences shewn anatomically between the figures of the king and his wife in the group PL. I, 1 ; however much good living and luxurious habits may have plumped his figure, it is distinctly that of a man, in contrast to his wife beside him. And the death-mask (PL. I, 10) cannot possibly be accepted as that of a woman. It is needless to further consider these fantastic hypotheses, which are flatly contradicted by every distinctive fact.

88. The monuments and deductions then of historical importance are as follow ; the age of the king is also added, according to what seems to be probable from the date of his marriage. The intermediate facts may belong to either the year placed before them or after them.

Age.	Reign.	
12	1	Accession. Thyi sole regent (Pl. XLII).
		Beginning of work at T. Amarna. North town (?).
		Villiers Stuart's tomb begun.
16	4	Married to Nefertythi.
		Cup (PL. XIII, 23).
		Conversion to Aten worship.
		Merytaten born.
		Scarab of Amenhotep adoring Aten (F. P. collection).
17	5	Latest document of Amenhotep IV. (Gurob).
		Change of name at Tell el Amarna.
18	6	Steles of Tell el Amarna, with one daughter.
		Maktaten born.
		Steles T. A., with two daughters.
		Theban work with two daughters (Pr. XI, 3).
		Change of name at Thebes.
		Theban work on young type still (Pr. X, 1).
		Change of face at Thebes (Pr. X, 2).
20	8	Steles T. A. with two daughters.
		Ankhnespa-aten born.
22 about	10	Nefer-neferu-aten-ta-shera born.
24 ,,	12	Nefer-neferu-aten born.
26 ,,	14	Setep-en-aten born.
28 ,,	16	Baqt-aten born.
29 ,,	17	Latest vintage date on jars.
		Association of Ra-smenkh-ka-ser-kheperu.
30 ,,	18	Death of Akhenaten.
		Desertion of the palace about a year later.

We see then that the name of Amenhotep and the previous type of face lasted longer at Thebes than elsewhere, as might be expected ; and that the chronology, the births of the children, and the length of reign nowhere shew any discordance. The later details we shall notice further on.

89. We now turn to the question of the portraiture; Whence came this remarkable type of Akhenaten? that the later style of his face was not derived from that of his father is obvious. But two heads of an aged queen were found among the trial-pieces; one is with the royal uraeus, the other is plain, but in better condition, (I, 6). These must evidently be of Thyi, as the face is too old and too dissimilar to be that of Nefertythi. Here the resemblance to Akhenaten is obvious (see I, 10); the same forehead almost in line with the nose, the same dreamy eye, the same delicate nose, the same expression of lips, the same long chin, the same slanting neck. That the boy inherited his face from his father (see I, 3, 7) cannot be doubted; and that he grew up like his mother seems equally clear.

Whether Thyi is the princess of Mitanni, named as a wife of Amenhotep III on the cuneiform correspondence, is not clear. The unintelligible allusion to Yuaa and Thuaa on the marriage scarab is a matter of dispute. But it is at least certain that Amenhotep III had Mesopotamian wives; and in a figure of a man of Mitanni, from the town of Ianua conquered by Ramessu II, we see exactly the same physiognomy as in Thyi and Akhenaten (I, 2). The precise points which have just been noted as being characteristic of the mother and son, are all seen here in this man, who might be almost supposed to have been drawn from Akhenaten himself (see I, 2; 9; 10. The source then of this peculiar face is the Mitannian blood of his mother Thyi.

90. So far I have treated the death-mask (see Frontispiece, and I, 10) as being from the head of Akhenaten. But it is as well to state the evidences for this attribution: as the cast is only a plaster casting, rough on the back, and without any name or mark. That it is a death-mask, and not modelled by hand, is shewn by the delicacy of the curves of the bone, by the flattening of the ear in casting, by the absence of modelled detail in the lips, and by the similar absence of detail in the eye, reinforced however by added lines done by a graving-tool to make it clearer. In all these points it is clearly not made by hand. The fillet on the head was to keep back the hair in casting. The cast comprises just as much of the face (going round to complete the mouth and eyes) as can be taken in one casting. That it was produced from an actual cast taken from the body is the unhesitating opinion of those who have had expe-

rience of such work, including the sculptor Mr. Alfred Gilbert. That the mould was cast on the dead body is shewn by the absence of any breathing-holes at either nostril or mouth, and by a trace of the open eyelid, distinguishable beside the graved lines of touching up.

We have then a cast taken after death, as a model for sculptors; a thing not known to have been done for any other king, and certainly shewing a care and an elaboration of work not likely for any but a very important person. No king died at Tell el Amarna beside Akhenaten. This cast bears an exact resemblance to the portraits of Akhenaten, and is a *via media* between the typical styles of his face as a boy and as a man; it reconciles the two in a manner which nothing but the original head would be likely to do. Further, this is found at a place where a great quantity of granite work has been prepared, and where many ushabtis of granite have been made, and cast aside, broken in working. And granite ushabtis of similar form are found in Akhenaten's tomb; while such are very rare, if not unknown, in any other place. Certainly no portrait bust of any Roman emperor has a better chain of evidence for its identification.

91. In the head of a princess, I, 11, there is a reversion to the type of her father as a boy, and her grandfather Amenhotep III. The fresco of the young princesses (I, 12) has been already noticed in sect. 27, and is more interesting artistically than as portraiture.

The queen Nefertythi had also a very marked personality. Portraits of her are as unmistakeable as those of Akhenaten. From the many statues of fine stone which existed in the temple, one fragment of nose and lips preserves to us a brilliant portrait (I, 15). The vivacity and strength of the work is unsurpassed in any period in Egypt; it has not the naive naturalness of the simple early work, but its conventions are all used to the best effect; the slight oversharpness of the edges of the lips gives a crispness and a clearness of shadow, which is most serviceable. The resemblance to the relief portraits, as in I, 14, is manifest. A torso of the same queen from the temple (I, 13) shews the same brilliant finish, and the combination of convention and naturalism in the treatment of the collar bone and bosom.

92. While referring to plate I, we may mention the other figures there. The piece of a stele, 16, is the most curious picture of domestic life in Egypt. Not content with representing the queen constantly associated with him, the king is here shewn seated, with

the queen on his knee, dancing her up and down on tiptoe. The grace of her feet drooping down, makes us more lament the loss of the heads. Between them are the two little princesses; one has been seated on the queen's right arm, the other has been dandled by the king, with her feet resting on the queen's lap. Behind the queen is a circular dish in four compartments filled with grapes, figs, and pomegranates, and a bouquet of lotus thrown over the top. The two horses' heads shew remarkable spirit and ability, though neither of them are more than sketches; No. 4 is drawn in black brush-work, with many other figures on a rough red pot. The hawk appears to have been added after the horse was drawn, the horse's neck being used to form the crown on the hawk's head, in an inexact shape. The head in relief, No. 8, is roughed out on the back of the piece with Akhenaten's head, No. 9.

93. The new style, which we have seen to be introduced by Akhenaten, was a revolution in art, in religion, and in ethics; and the personality of a man who could make such a prodigious change in the short space of a few years, is indeed one of the most fascinating studies in history. The key-note of all his motives is to be seen in his favourite motto, which was repeated on all his monuments, and prefixed to both of his cartouches, a prominence that no other king gave to any expression. This motto was not one of violence, of valour, or of power, abroad; nor of glory, or ostentation, at home; it was the unique and philosophic phrase "*Ankh em maat,*" "Living in the Truth." As we look into his new views and ways we shall see how plainly this was his leading thought, how he aimed in everything to attain truth, and to live in a true spirit. In the hymn to the Aten Ay calls Akhenaten "the Prince of Truth" as his first title.

The most distinctive and novel feature of the religion of Akhenaten was the prominent place given to the rays of the sun. In every sculpture the rays are the main feature, rays ending in hands which act, to give life to each person, and to accept offerings from each. In the hymn to the Aten Ay repeatedly mentions the rays and radiation: "thou pourest rays on thy son who loves thee, thy hands filled with millions of festivals"; Akhenaten is the "son of the sun, who exalts his beauties, who presents to him the product of his rays"; he is "embraced by his rays." This is an idea not found in any other period; an express appreciation of the power of the radiant energy of the sun, apparently in opposition to the idea of the sun being only a distant intangible mass.

Just as the older Ra worship of the sun as a personal deity, was completely abandoned and set aside, with all human or animal representations of the deity, and a new name, the Aten, was adopted to break the anthropomorphic connection of thought; so in the same manner the disc was kept apart from the notion of being an intangible supernatural personality, and its rays which act amongst men and give life are the special object of representation. This distinction of the thought of rays as emitted and apart from the source is very peculiar. In no sun worship have the rays been so clearly appreciated as the source of life and action; and the distinction thus made shews a keener realising of the scientific distinction between source and rays, and of the real importance of the rays to men, than has ever been touched until perhaps the present century. It was a reaching forward to the truth with a truly philosophic view and determination, which anticipated the course of thought some thousands of years.

94. "Living in the Truth" was his motto in art, as well as in religion. The new style of sculpture and of painting is marked by the fullest naturalism. The careful delicacy of expression in the faces of the king (I, 5, 9), and the queen (I, 15), the spirit of the fresco of the princesses (I, 12), the vigour of the horses' heads (I, 4, 8), the copying of rapid motion in the calves (III, 3; IV, 4, 5), the natural grace of the plants (III, IV), all of these shew the eager grasping after truth in art, which opened a new field of ideas.

95. And again in ethics the departure is as wide. No other king ever dedicated himself to an ethical idea as Akhenaten did; when he was a boy, Maat sits by him protecting him; as a man he puts the ideal forward on all occasions, he "lives in Truth." The attainment and spread of truth was the object of his life. In the details of private life the same aim at truth is seen. He, truly devoted to his one queen, is not ashamed of whatever is the truth, and he appears with her on all occasions; he is determined not to suppress anything, but openly kisses the queen as they ride in a chariot, and dances her on his knee with the babies as he sits on a throne. His domestic affection is the truth, and as the truth he proclaims it. Here is a revolution in ideas! No king of Egypt, nor of any other part of the world, has ever carried out his honesty of expression so openly. His domestic life was his ideal of the truth of life, and as part of his living in truth he proclaims it as the true life to his subjects.

Thus in every line Akhenaten stands out as perhaps the most original thinker that ever lived in Egypt, and one of the great idealists of the world.

No man appears to have made a greater stride to a new standpoint than he did, from the plundering, self-glorifying, pompous cruelty of his conquering fore-fathers, to the abstract devotion to the truth in each department of life, and the steadfast determination to advance the following of the truth with all the powers of his position.

96. The length of Akhenaten's reign has been hitherto quite unknown on the monuments, none bearing a higher date than the 8th year. From the large series of inscriptions on wine jars, however, we reach firm ground; and as they were collected from many different parts of the town they are not likely to be restricted to any one part of the reign. In Mr. Griffith's Chapter V, the details are given; and when we see a continuous series of inscriptions of every year, from Akhenaten's occupation of the site onwards, varying from two to eleven examples each year, and then find an absolute cessation at the seventeenth year, it is almost certain that he must have died before the eighteenth vintage. The 37 years given by Manetho and Josephus may then refer to the duration of the Aten worship, including the reign of Ra-smenkh-ka-ser-khepru, and part of that of Tut-ankh-amen. Further, the number of his daughters agree well to the shorter duration of his reign. And the features of the death-mask are those of a young man: different estimates put the age of that at about thirty years old, or between thirty and forty. From the chronology already given it seems probable that Akhenaten died at about thirty, and it thus agrees well with the age shewn by the mask.

97. His successor Ra-smenkh-ka-ser-khepru appears to have been associated in the kingdom. He has often the title "beloved of Ra-nefer-kheperu" or "beloved of Ua-n-ra"; the rings with such titles are of good work like those of Akhenaten (XV, 92–96), and not like Ra-smenkh-ka's simpler ones, which are much inferior (97–102). These seem to have been made closely connected with those of Akhenaten, and while his successor was dependent on him. Again, Mery-taten the eldest daughter was born probably in the close of the fourth year of her father's reign, and would therefore be full thirteen years old at the close of his seventeenth regnal year, at which time Ra-smenkh-ka-sar-kheperu may well have married her, and been associated as the king's son-in-law and successor. These co-regency rings are mainly found in the palace waste heaps, and nothing later than these belong there. Now we know that the great hall of the palace was deserted, and used for broken jars, in the second or third year of Ra-smenkh-ka, by the

dates found on the fragments. And this accords with his later, and independent type, of rings not being found in the waste which was carried out from the palace while it was used. The royal residence was therefore moved away from Tell el Amarna about a couple of years after Akhenaten's death; but the town still lasted for some time as a centre of manufactures and population. The ring factories continued to make rings of Ra-smenkh-ka; and, after him, under his successor Tut-ankh-amen the business was still active. But at this point the Aten was renounced; the double reading Amen or Aten on XV, 118 shews this, and there are many ostentatiously Amen-adoring rings of the later part of his reign.

It has been suggested that Tut-ankh-amen preceded Akhenaten; but in many ways the works of Tut-ankh-amen are distinctly intermediate between Akhenaten and Horemheb. The style of the rings, the colours of the glazes, the styles of the pendants and the beads, all shew a date later than Akhenaten. Nor is there any place in the succession of Manetho or Josephus for a king between Amenhotep III and IV. It is true that the style of the sculpture of Tut-ankh-amen does not shew any trace of the influence of Akhenaten; yet no more does the work of Horemheb or Seti I; and therefore no argument as to date can be founded on it. A strong evidence of the usual view followed by historians is in the name of the wife of Tut-ankh-amen. The first daughter of Akhenaten married Ra-smenkh-ka; the second daughter died young; the third was Ankh-s-en-pa-aten, and the wife of Tut-ankh-amen was Ankh-s-en-amen, apparently the same name changed. In Lieblein's dictionary there is not a single name of this type (Ankh-s(or f) en ——) in this period, not for some centuries later; hence it cannot have been a common name then, and the evidence for Tut-ankh-amen having been the son-in-law of Akhenaten is all the stronger.

98. But there are no rings at Tell el Amarna of later date than Tut-ankh-amen; and therefore it appears that the town was mainly deserted in his reign, and the factories moved elsewhere. As rings of Ay and Horemheb are found at Memphis, it seems likely that the industry moved to that centre. Of the reign of Ay there is no trace at Tell el Amarna; but the unfinished tomb there was probably made by him when he was a high courtier of Akhenaten. He was fanbearer at the king's right hand, director of the royal stud, and divine father; and his wife was Thy, nurse to Nefertythi. His tomb is one of the finest in the place, both for size and workmanship;

and it is evident that he was one of the most powerful subjects, his wife being also in high office. When we next see the divine father Ay as king, with a queen Thy, it is presumably the same person. The only objection is that the king had a tomb at Thebes, and the official had one at Tell el Amarna; as however the official's tomb has no funeral chamber, and has never been finished, it is quite likely that he deserted it, and began his Theban tomb when he reached the throne.

There is, strangely, a stone of Horemheb, found in the west end of the great temenos (PL. XI, 5), broken from a piece of finished and coloured sculpture, and therefore not done as a freak by some workman. From the curve of the top of the cartouche it is clear that it cannot have contained more than *Ra* above the *ser-kheperu*; and Horemheb has the titles *heq-maat*, *heq-uas*, and *heq-an*. This cannot have been then the name Ra-smenkh-ka-ser-kheperu; but the question is still open, if that king was not identical with Horemheb, and simplified his cartouche in his later times. As however Nezem-mut (Nefertythi's sister) would probably be married not very long after Nefertythi, and is probably the same as Horemheb's queen, it is not likely that Ra-smenkh-ka who married Merytaten can be the same as Horemheb who married Nezem-mut. After Horemheb there is not a single royal name found at Tell el Amarna.

99. We will now see how far questions remain open. Akhenaten was certainly succeeded by his son-in-law, and probable co-regent, Ra-smenkh-ka, as the rings and vases of the latter are the only later ones found in the palace and palace rubbish, and he is called "beloved of Akhenaten." Ay certainly did not come before Tut-ankh-amen, as he is never found in the factories which abound with Tut-ankh-amen's work. Neither was he contemporary with Tut-ankh-amen, as the latter reigned long and powerfully at Thebes, and Ay's tomb is at Thebes; and shews lengthy work. The succession then was Akhenaten, Ra-smenkh-ka, Tut-ankh-amen, and Ay. As Horemheb has usurped a block of Tut-ankh-amen (Denk. III, 119 b), and also of Ay, in the Karnak pylon, it is certain that he was later than both of those kings.

If we attempt any chronology of this period, we might adopt the 12 years which Josephus gives to the daughter of Akhenaten (Horos), for Ra-smenkh-ka the daughter's husband; also the 9 years Josephus gives for her brother, Ratothis, may be the reign of her brother-in-law Tut-ankh-amen, who married the third daughter, Ankh-s-en-pa-aten (the second having

died young): there is then apparently a duplication of the reign of Ay (both the name and the reign being repeated) which gives 12 years. Lastly, Horemheb has only 4 years as Armais in Josephus, and his 21 years on the monuments refers probably to a period during which he was partly independent as a successful general abroad. We have then:—

Akhenaten	18 years.
Ra-smenkh-ka-ser-kheperu . . .	12 ,,
Tut-ankh-amen	9 ,,
Ay	12 ,,
Horembeb	4 ,,

There are two presumable checks on this. First, the 36 years given to Akhenaten by the lists cannot be his actual reign, as we find that to be only 17 or 18 years; it is therefore probably the duration of his new worship, which we have seen comes to an end under Tut-ankh-amen. And the 36 years would end in the sixth year of this king, leaving 3 years for his Amen worship. Next, it is probable that Nezem-mut. the sister of Nefertythi, is also the wife of Horemheb. If so, taking the sister at 4 years younger than Nefertythi (perhaps more, perhaps less), she would be married at about the fifth year of Akhenaten; if she were then 15 years old she would be 65 at the death of her husband, Horemheb, a result which is not at all unlikely.

100. The idea that Tell el Amarna was rapidly deserted and destroyed in a year or two after the death of Akhenaten, does not seem borne out by the data. If this were so we must altogether abandon the reigns given by Manetho and Josephus; they are bad and corrupt no doubt, but cannot be quite set aside. But a more solid reason is seen in the factories of the town. In considering the number of dated rings, etc., we may regard either the total number of objects or the number of varieties of moulds used. The following are the numbers of moulds, and of moulded pieces, whole or broken, obtained by me in 1891–2.

	Total Numbers.			Varieties.		
	Objects.	Moulds.	All.	Objects.	Moulds.	All.
Akhenaten	72	54	126	47	19	56
The Aten	22	36	58	21	10	26
Nefertythi.	9	35	44	6	3	8
Ankhsen-pa-aten . . .	10	..	10	2	..	2
Ra-smenkh-ka . . .	43	4	47	19	3	22
Merytaten.	5	..	5	2	..	2
Tut-ankh-amen — before Amen.	15	11	26	9	8	13
Tut-ankh-amen — with Amen.	12	3	15	3	3	4

Here we see that whether we regard the total number of objects, or the number of varieties, Ra-smenkh-ka (who only lived at Tell el Amarna two or three years in place of Akhenaten's twelve years) has between a third and a half of the numbers of Akhenaten. And Tut-ankh-amen is nearly as well represented as Ra-smenkh-ka. Allowing for the absence of any palace rubbish (which was the greatest supply of Akhenaten's objects), the proportion of objects of Ra-smenkh-ka and of Tut-ankh-amen is quite as large in proportion to the length of reigns as that of Akhenaten's. Hence the activity of the factories shews that it is very unlikely that they ceased in two or three years after Akhenaten; on the contrary it agrees well with the length of reigns of his successors given by Josephus. The proportion of the Amen objects in those of Tut-ankh-amen also agrees closely with the proportion of years just named by the chronology. From that I suggested that 6 years were on the Aten system, and the remaining 3 on the Amen system: and we see that the proportion of the total numbers is about 2 to 1, and of varieties 3 to 1, which is a remarkable agreement for a method which is only approximate.

101. The worship of Aten being abandoned then about eighteen years after Akhenaten's death, the purpose of the town as a religious centre ceased. Yet the population did not leave it; the number of Amen rings seems to shew that until the death of Tut-ankh-amen the factories still continued. Then comes a blank, when the town appears to have been rapidly deserted. Yet the Aten worship was not proscribed, and the priests appear on the accession of Horemheb to have put up his name on the existing buildings, from the fragment (XI, 5) which was found.

But Horemheb finally abolished the Aten worship. His pylon at Thebes is built of the blocks of Akhenaten's Theban buildings; and he seems to have rapidly removed everything at Tell el Amarna. Not only the stone buildings, but their very foundations were eradicated; in all our work there was not one stone left in its place that was large enough to be worth using; a few patches of mortar and small stones were the whole remains *in situ*. This proves that the destruction was very rapid and systematic. When a building is only resorted to for stone as required, the upper parts are ruined first, chips accumulate, and the foundations, and perhaps the lower courses, are so encumbered as not to be worth extraction. But here the clearance must have been made systematically, clearing out one part thoroughly before going further. And with this accords also the erasure of the Aten, and the names of Akhenaten and the queen, on most of the rock monuments. Akhenaten in his new zeal had erased the name of Amen from end to end of Egypt; and now the revenge came of erasing the Aten worship and its founder, from the face of the land, and from the page of history. All the new ideals, the "living in the truth," the veneration of the rays, the naturalism in art, the ethical views, all melted away, without leaving perceptible trace on the minds and ways of the Egyptians; and they rushed on into an age of warfare and decadence. Horemheb seems to have deported all the stone of Tell el Amarna, and used it for foundations and building throughout the lower country; at Memphis, at Heliopolis, great quantities of these remains have been found; and considering the immense amount that was removed from Tell el Amarna, there is as yet no proof that the remains of Akhenaten in other places shew that he built elsewhere below Thebes; but only that Horemheb, and perhaps Seti I, had brought their stone away from the capital. Akhenaten's oath not to leave Tell el Amarna, suggests that he limited his work to that place.

102. Such was the fall of one of the great movements of human thought, carried out by a single idealist, who set himself against the traditions, the religion, and the habits of his country. Even his royal position might not have enabled him to make such a change, had he not possessed a character of boldness and extreme tenacity—perhaps a dreamy obstinacy—with much delicacy of feeling, kindness of manner, a sense of humour, and a pleasure in popular enjoyments. All this may be seen in his face—his very own face that we have preserved in the death-mask, apart from all transcription. In his remarkable position, the greatness of his changes, the modernity of his thoughts, the wreck of his ideas, this strange humanist is one of the most fascinating characters of history; and into his face we can now look, as if we had seen him in the flesh.

INDEX.

LONDON : PRINTED BY WILLIAM CLOWES AND SONS, LIMITED, STAMFORD STREET AND CHARING CROSS.

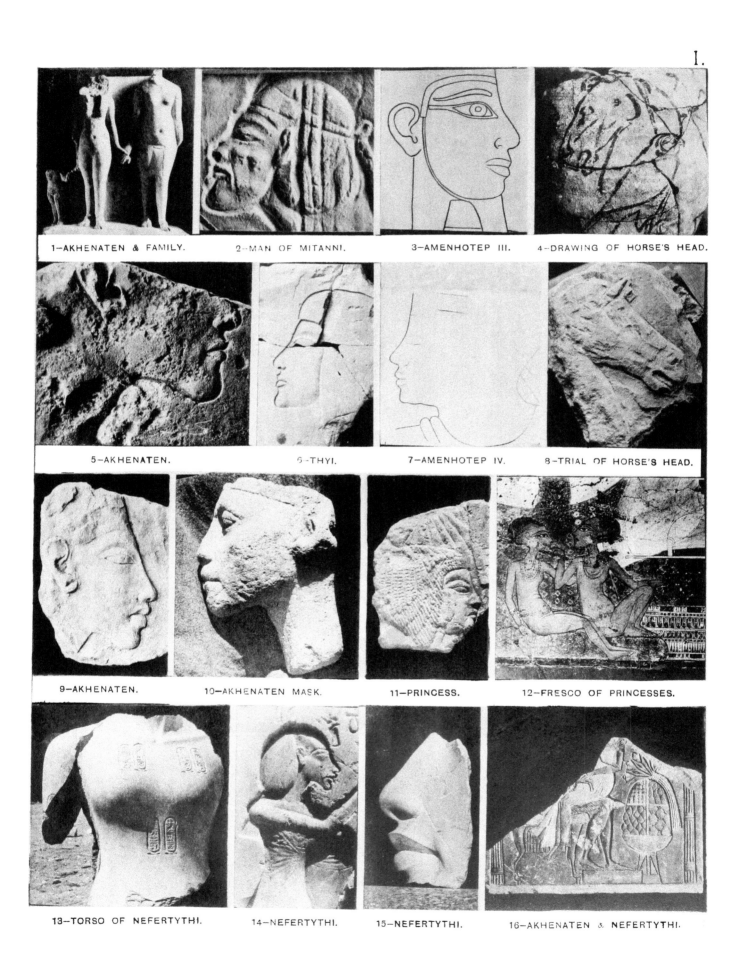

1—AKHENATEN & FAMILY. 2—MAN OF MITANNI. 3—AMENHOTEP III. 4—DRAWING OF HORSE'S HEAD.

5—AKHENATEN. 6—THYI. 7—AMENHOTEP IV. 8—TRIAL OF HORSE'S HEAD.

9—AKHENATEN. 10—AKHENATEN MASK. 11—PRINCESS. 12—FRESCO OF PRINCESSES.

13—TORSO OF NEFERTYTHI. 14—NEFERTYTHI. 15—NEFERTYTHI. 16—AKHENATEN & NEFERTYTHI.

TELL EL AMARNA. WEST HALF OF PAINTED PAVEMENT.

1:20.

The material originally positioned here is too large for reproduction in this reissue. A PDF can be downloaded from the web address given on page iv of this book, by clicking on 'Resources Available'.

1

2

3

1:10

1:2.

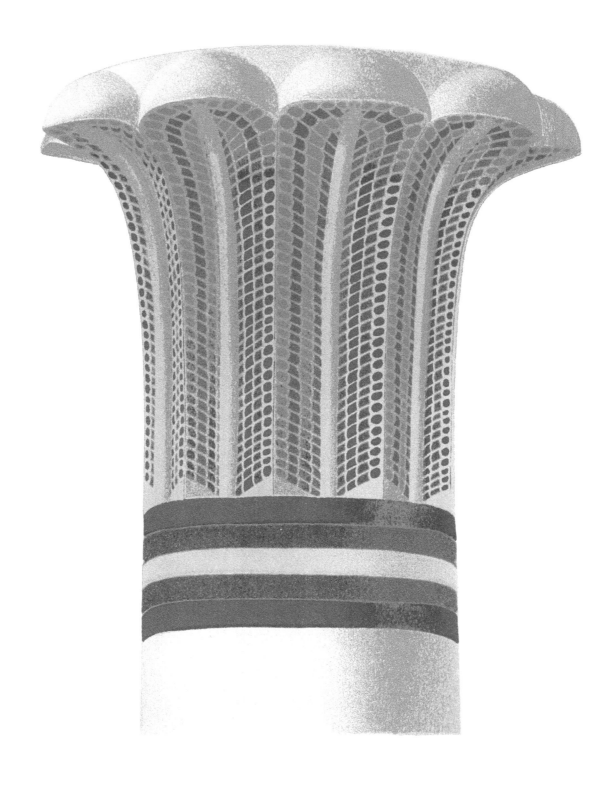

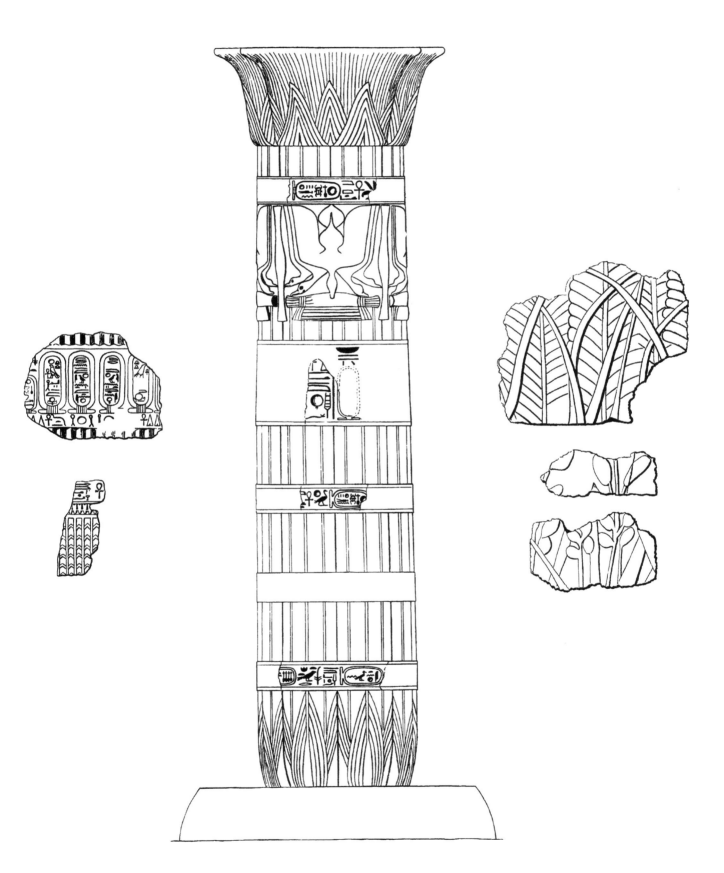

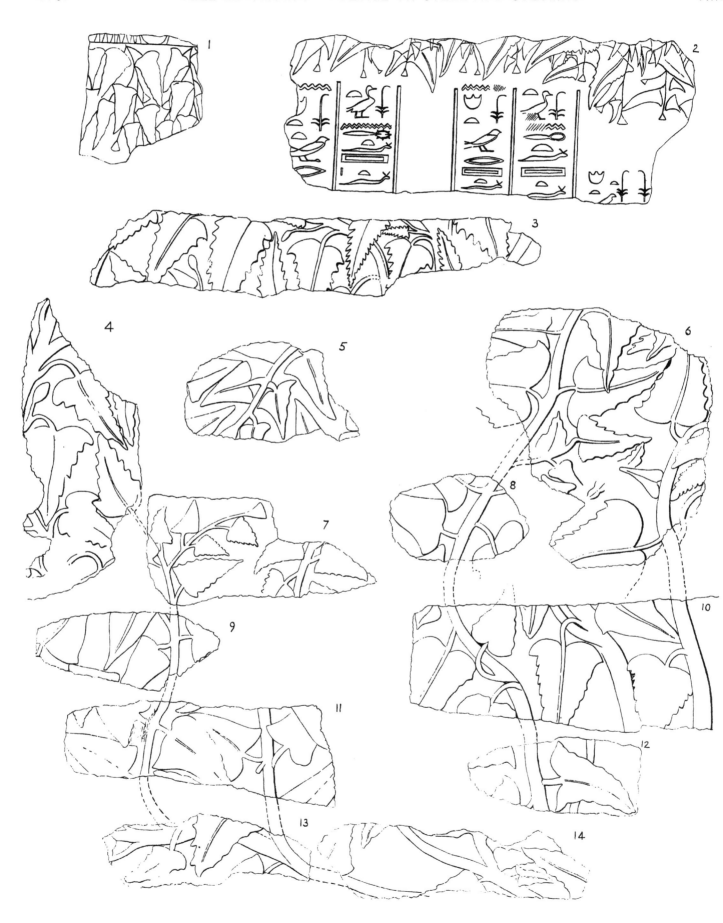

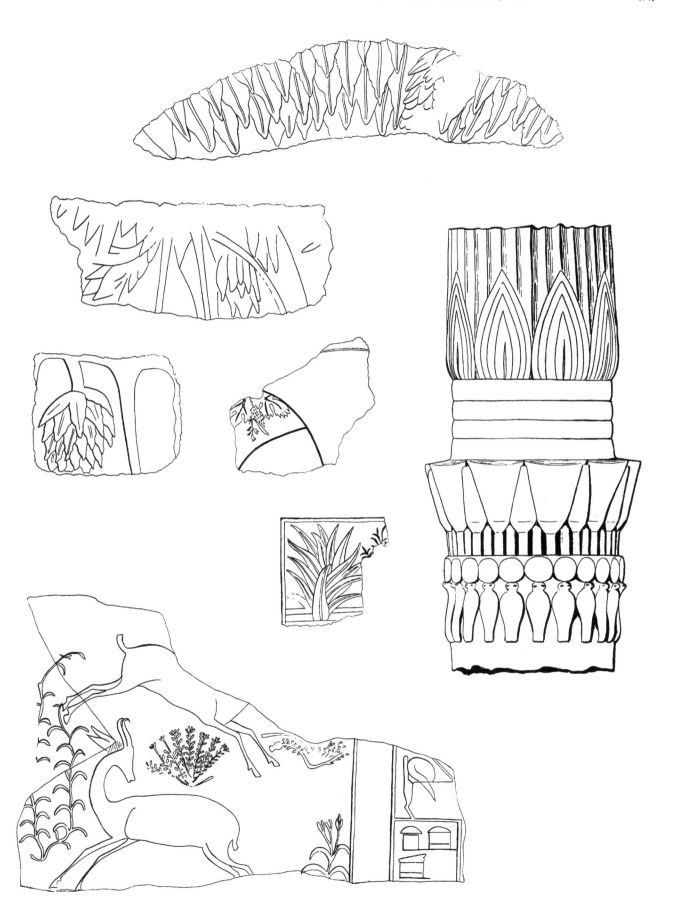

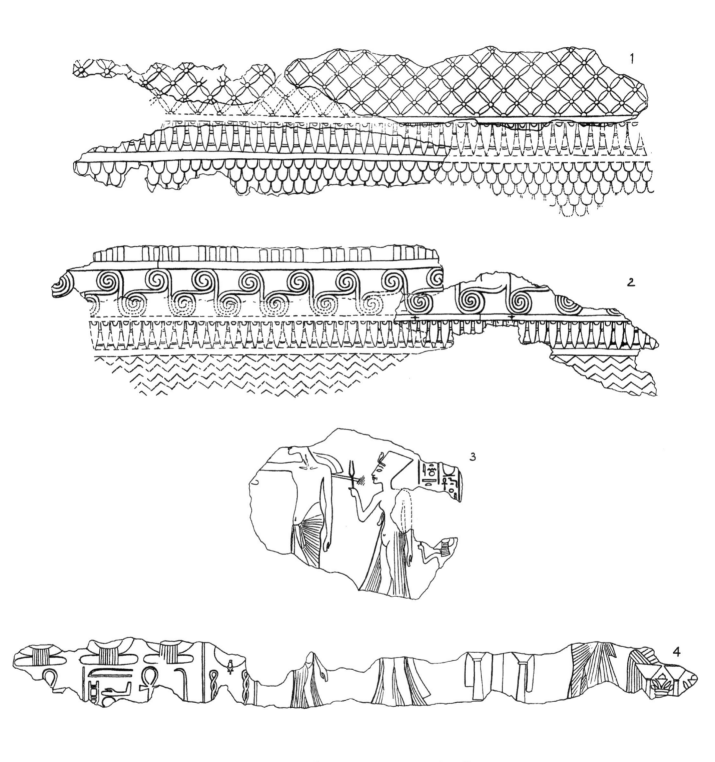

COPING OF WELL EDGE

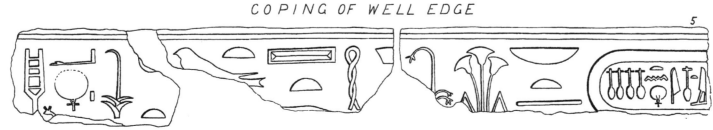

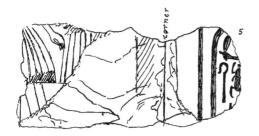

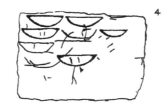

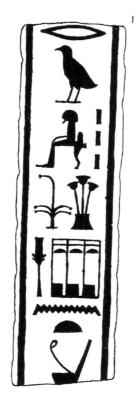

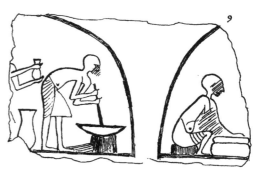

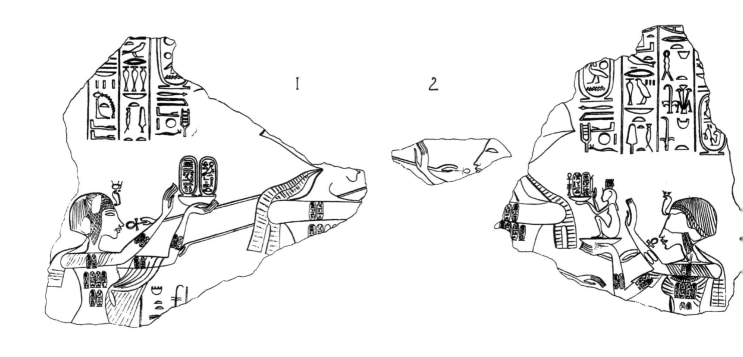

1

2

3

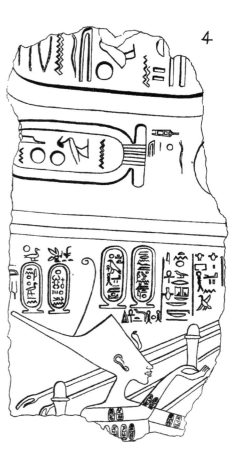

4

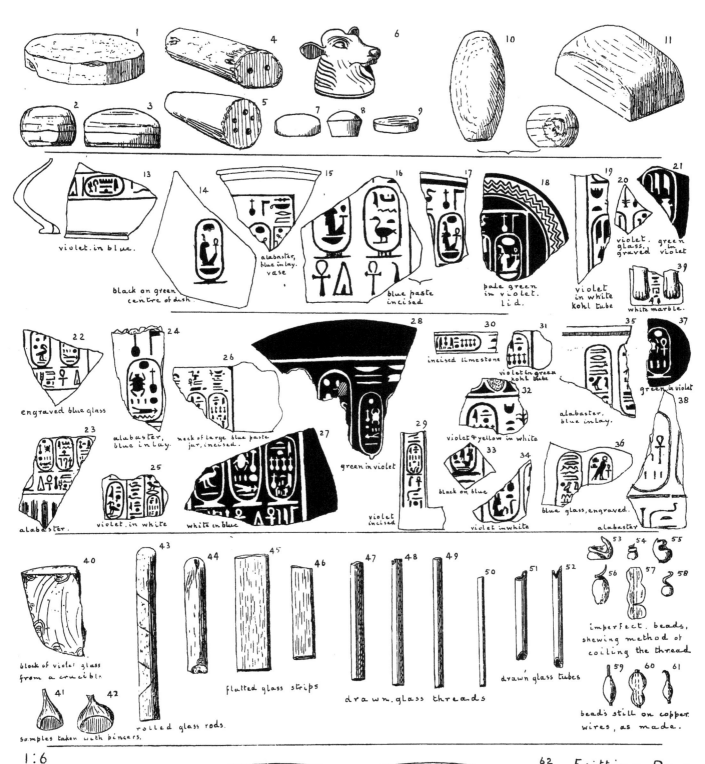

violet in blue.

black on green
centre of dish.

alabaster,
blue inlay.
vase

blue paste
incised

pale green
in violet.
lid.

violet glass,
graved

green
in
violet

violet
in white
kohl tube

white marble.

engraved blue glass

alabaster,
blue inlay.

neck of large blue paste
jar, incised.

green in violet

incised limestone

violet in green
kohl tube

violet & yellow in white

alabaster,
blue inlay.

green in violet

alabaster.

violet in white

white in blue

violet
incised

black on blue

violet in white

blue glass, engraved.

alabaster

block of violet glass
from a crucible.

samples taken with pincers.

rolled glass rods.

flatted glass strips

drawn glass threads

drawn glass tubes

imperfect beads,
shewing method of
coiling the thread

beads still on copper
wires, as made.

1:6

62   *Fritting Pans,*
supported in the
furnace on jars
inverted, down
which the glaze runs.

N.M.F.P.

TAHUTMES III.

AMENHOTEP III.

   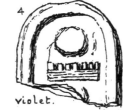

gn. sch.   bl. sch.   gn. sch.   violet.   br. burnt?   gn. bl.   gn. sch.   bl. gn.   bl. gn.

THYI.

bl.   bl.   bl.   gn.   lt. bl.   gn.   bl.   lt. gn.   lt. bl.   gn.

AMENHOTEP IV — AKHENATEN

violet glass   bl.

  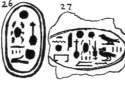

gn. sch.   gn. sch.   gn. sch.   bl. sch.   bl. sch.   M.   bl.   bl. M.   bl.   gn. bl.

gn.   bl.   bl.   bl. M.   bl.   bl. M   bl.   bl.   violet glass

   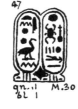   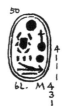 

bl. violet thick   bl. yell.   bl. M   bl. M   bl. M small large   bl.   bl.   violet   bl. violet   bl. faded

THE ATEN.

bl.   bl.   carnelian   limestone ring.   lt. bl. M.   bl. M large

M.2   M.2   gn. M24   gn. M.   bl. M.2   red. M.   bl.   bl.   yell.   yell.

ATEN-NEFER-NEFERU-NEFERT-YTHI. ANKH-S-EN-PA-ATEN.

RA-SMENKH-KA-SER-KHEPERU

ATEN-MERT. TUT-ANKH AMEN

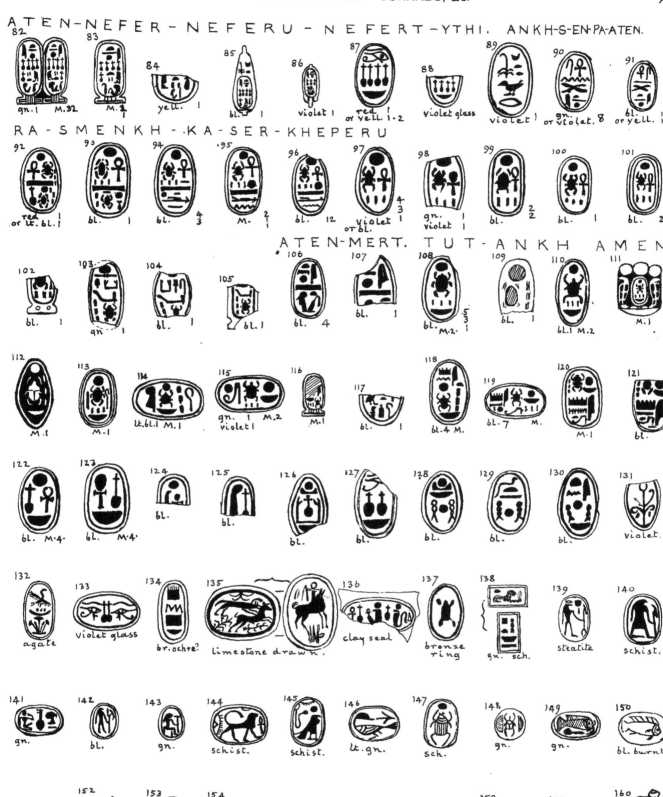

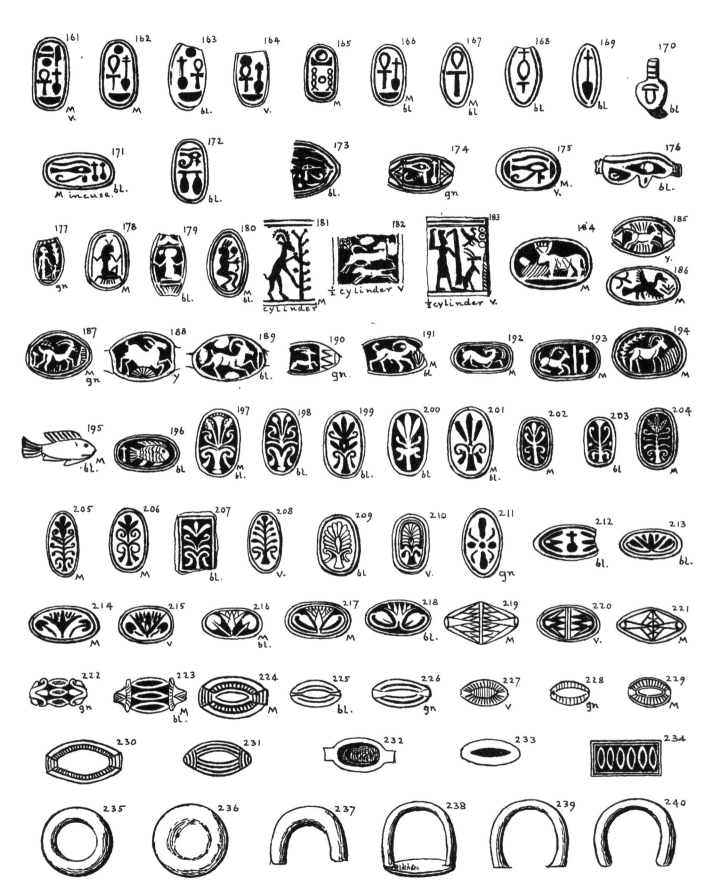

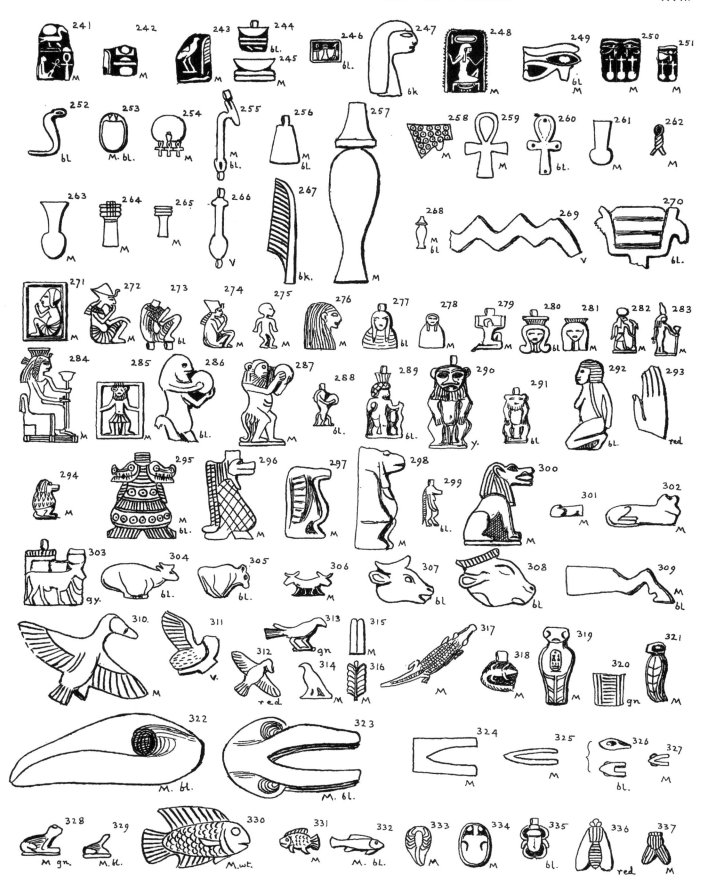

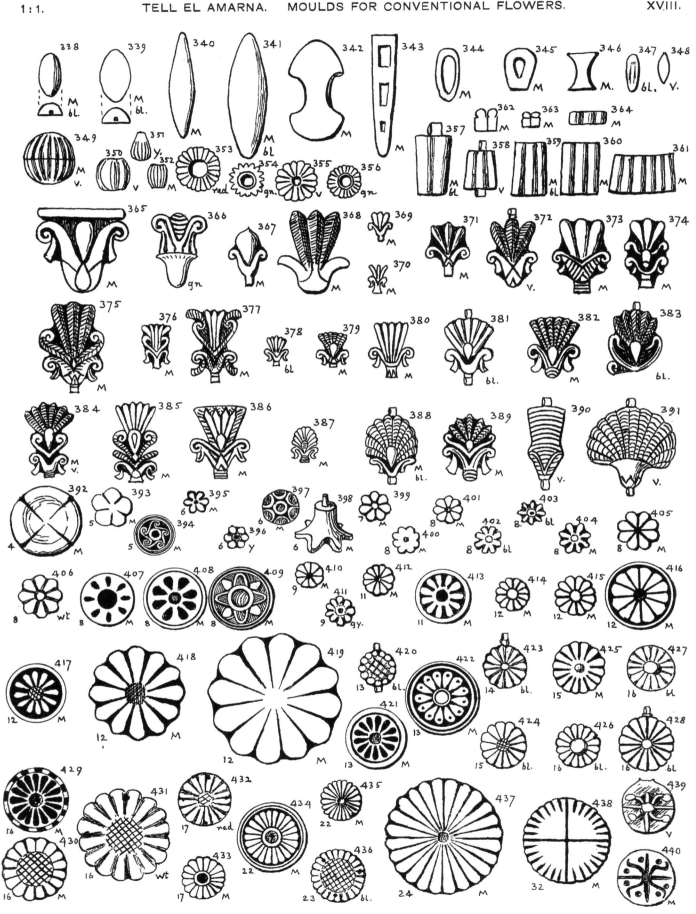

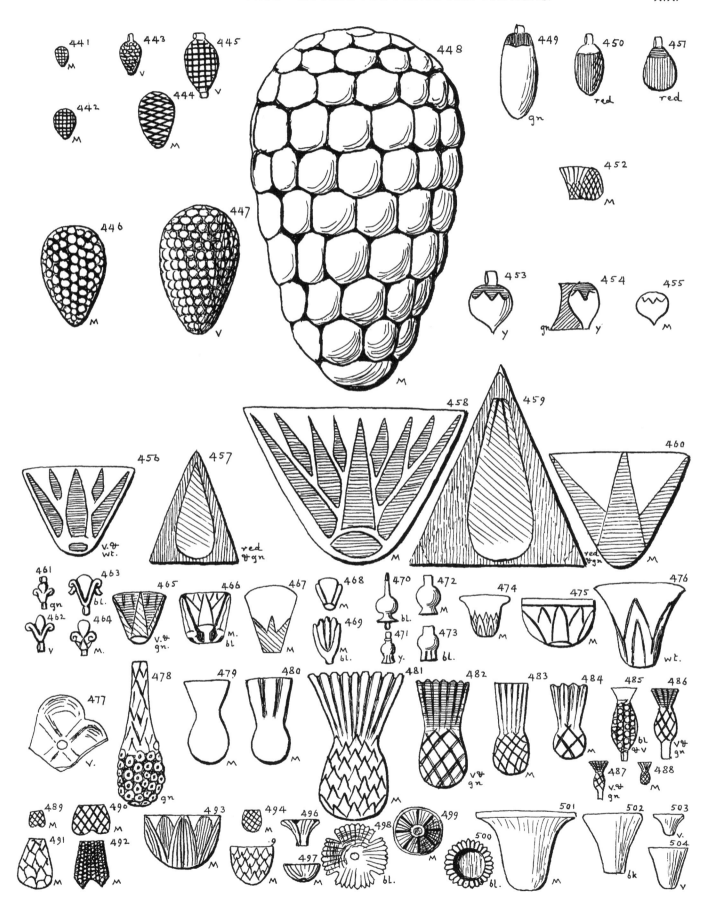

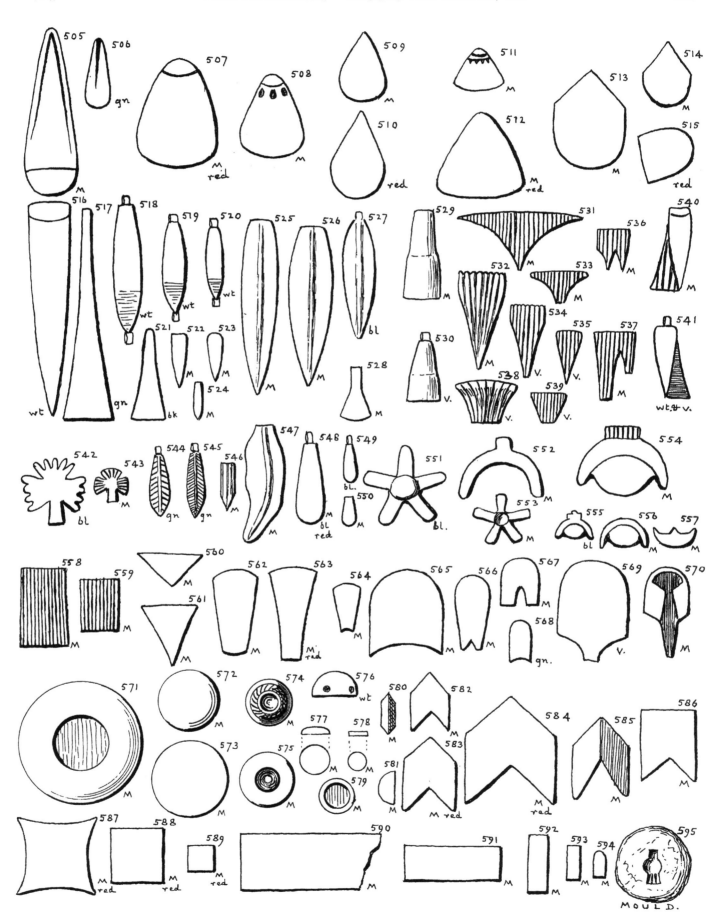

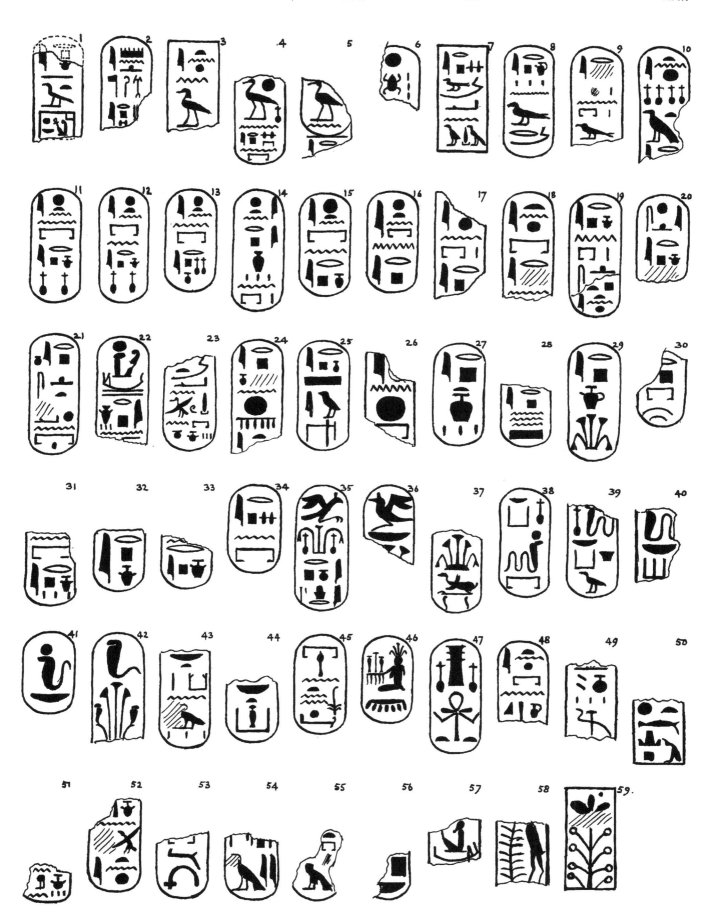

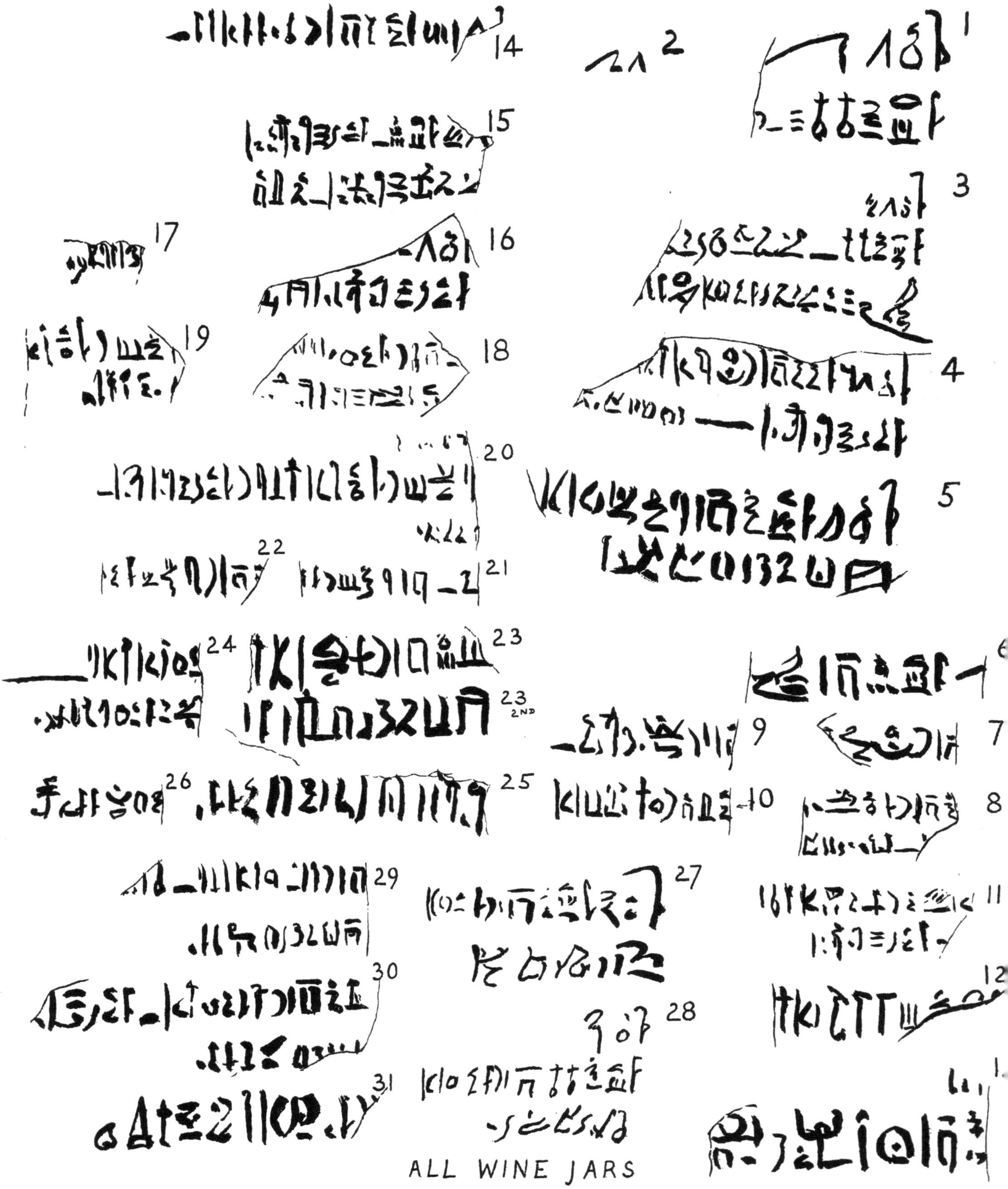

ALL WINE JARS

35

36

37

32

33

34

40

41

42

OIL

38

39

MEAT

47

48

50

49

52

51

54

53

57

44

45

43

46

55

56

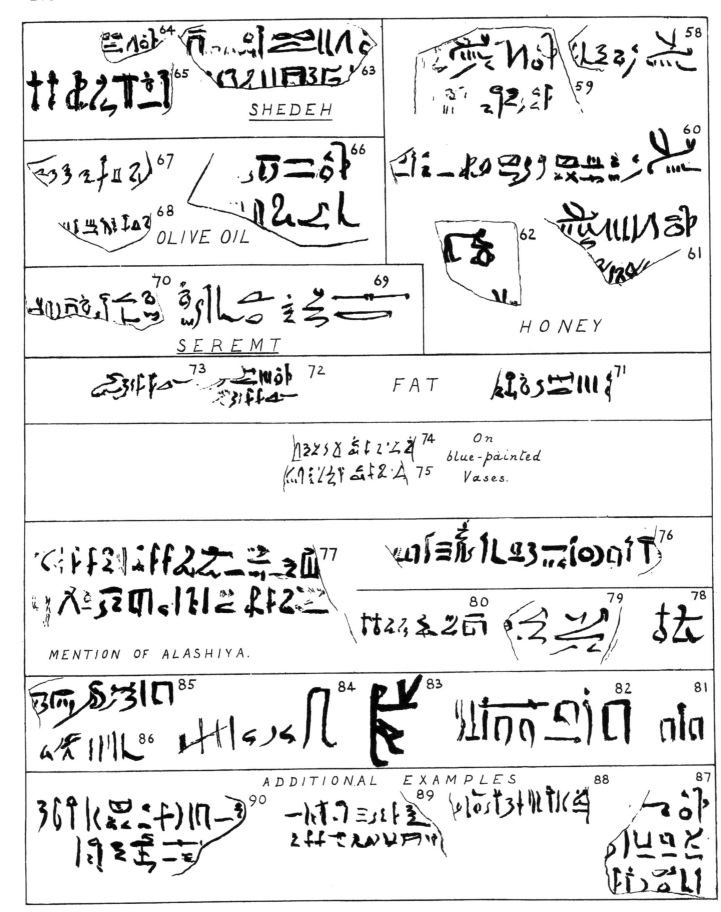

SHEDEH

OLIVE OIL

SEREMT

HONEY

FAT

On blue-painted Vases.

MENTION OF ALASHIYA.

ADDITIONAL EXAMPLES

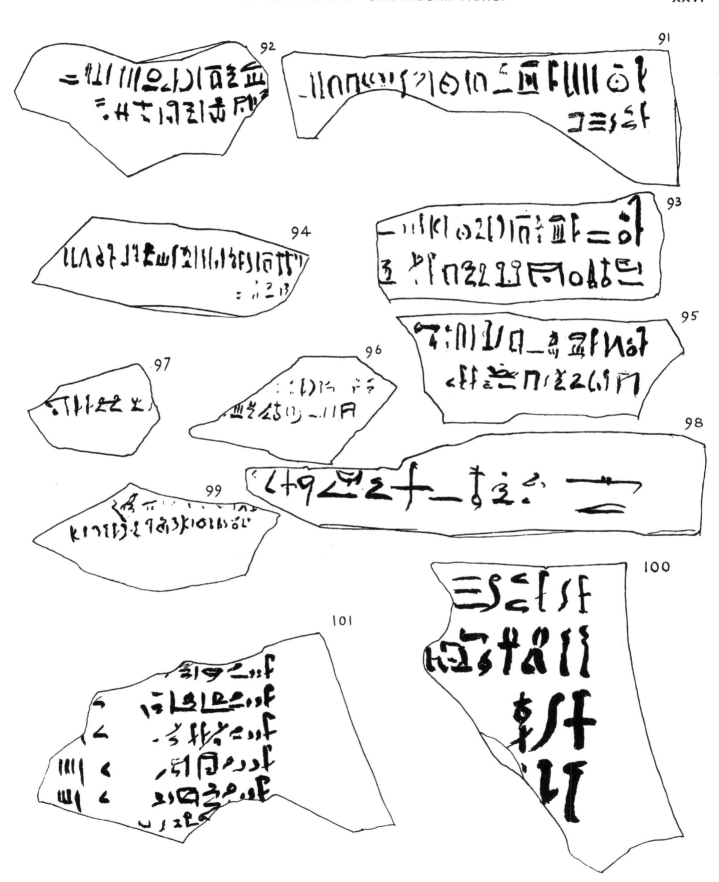

PYXIDES

BOWLS

WIDE NECKED PIRIFORM.

PIRIFORM VASES.

FALSE NECKED VASES.

House II

I.

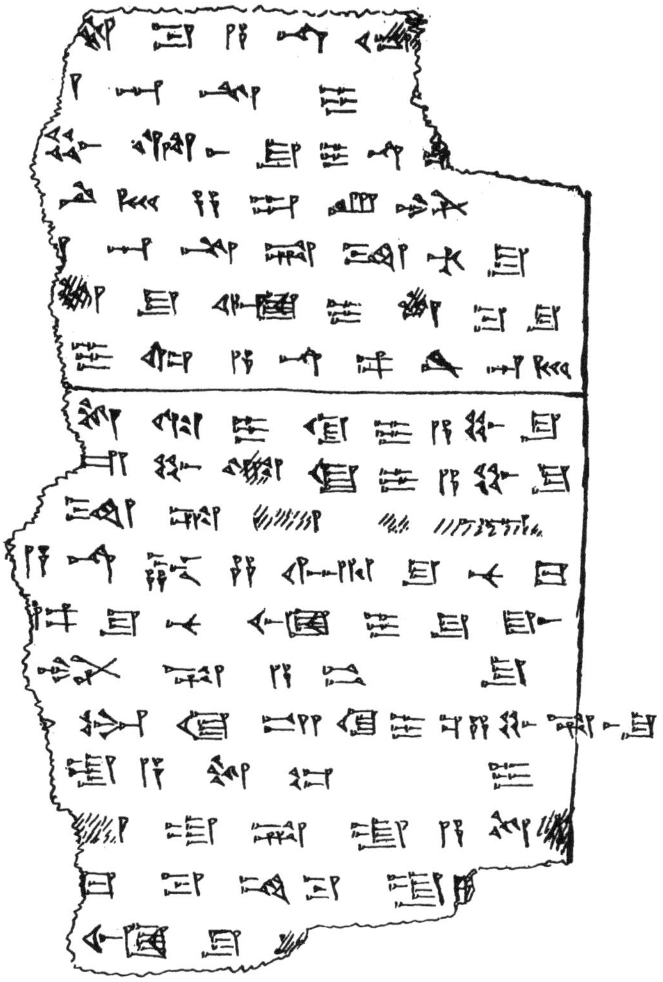

II.

Obverse:

Reverse:

Edge: 1. 2. 3. 4.

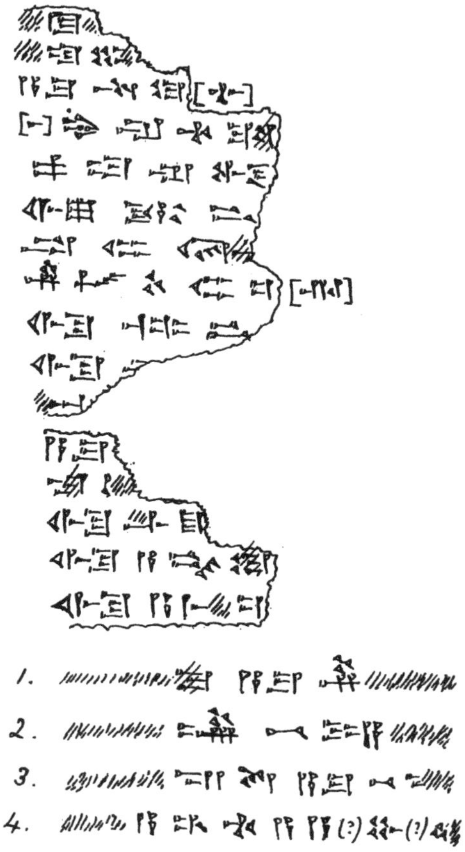

III

Obverse:

Reverse:

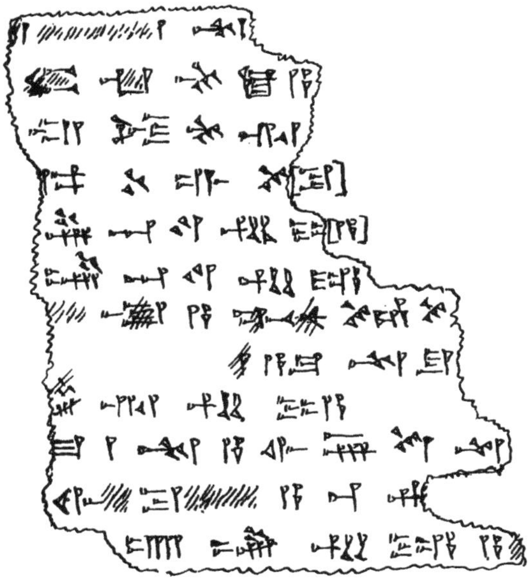

IV.

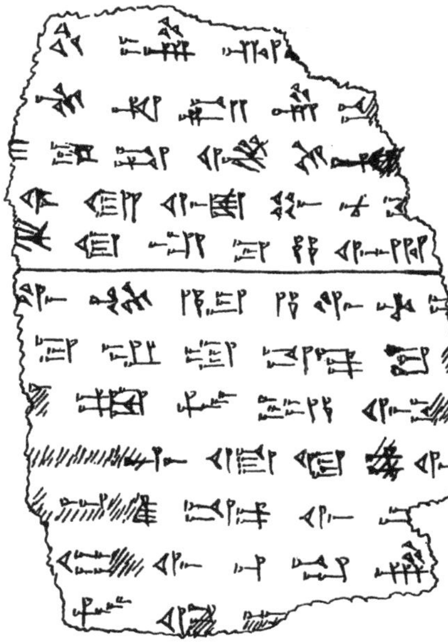

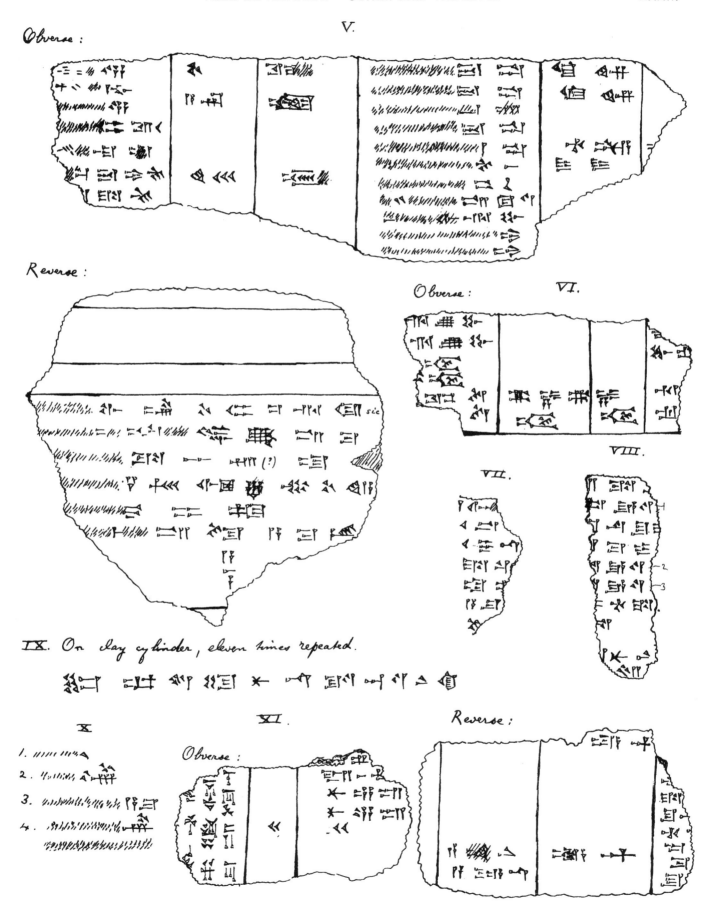

V.

Obverse :

Reverse :

Obverse :   VI.

VII.   VIII.

IX. On clay cylinder, eleven times repeated.

X

1.
2.
3.
4.

XI.

Obverse :   Reverse :

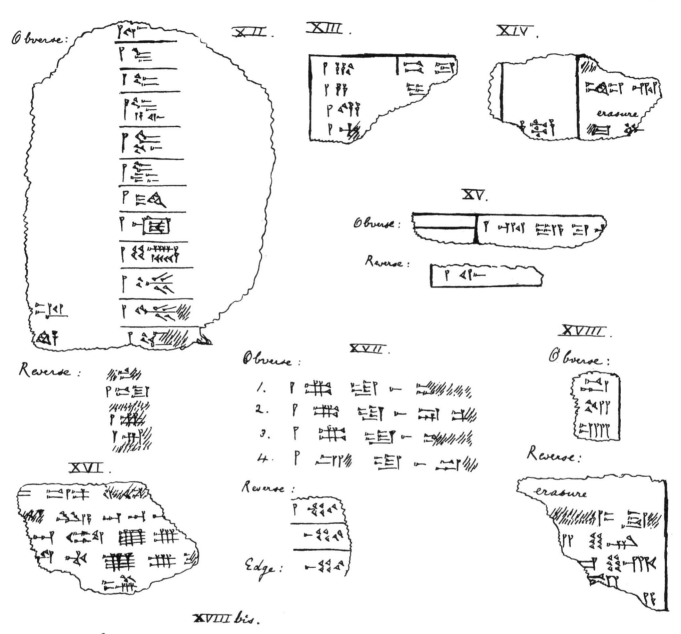

The material originally positioned here is too large for reproduction in this reissue. A PDF can be downloaded from the web address given on page iv of this book, by clicking on 'Resources Available'.

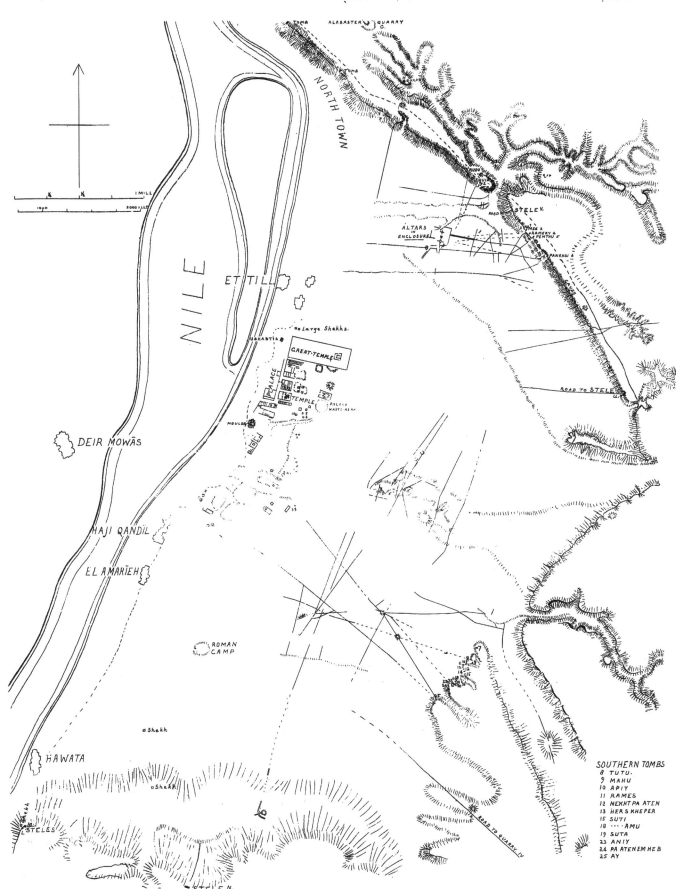

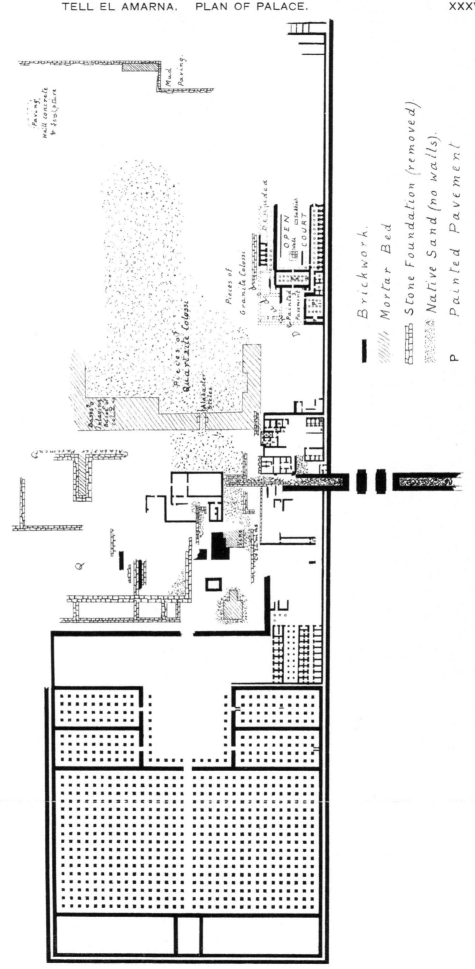

The material originally positioned here is too large for reproduction in this reissue. A PDF can be downloaded from the web address given on page iv of this book, by clicking on 'Resources Available'.

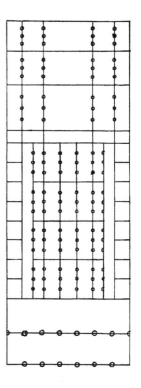

Plan in Quarry

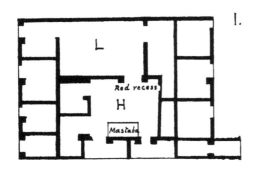

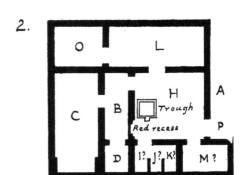

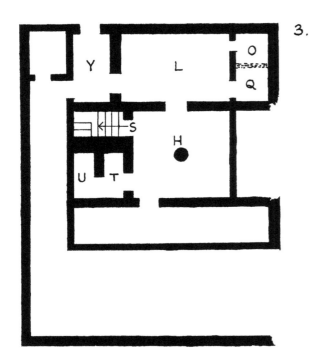

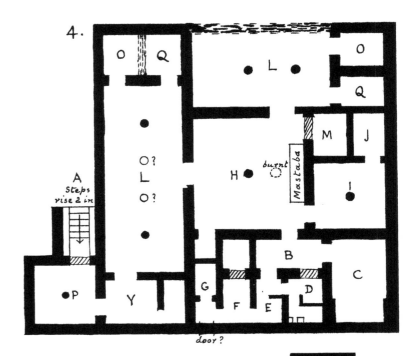

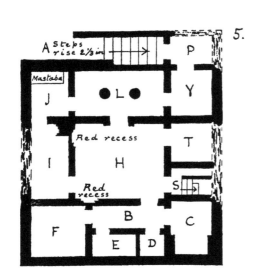

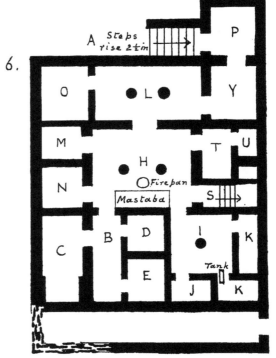

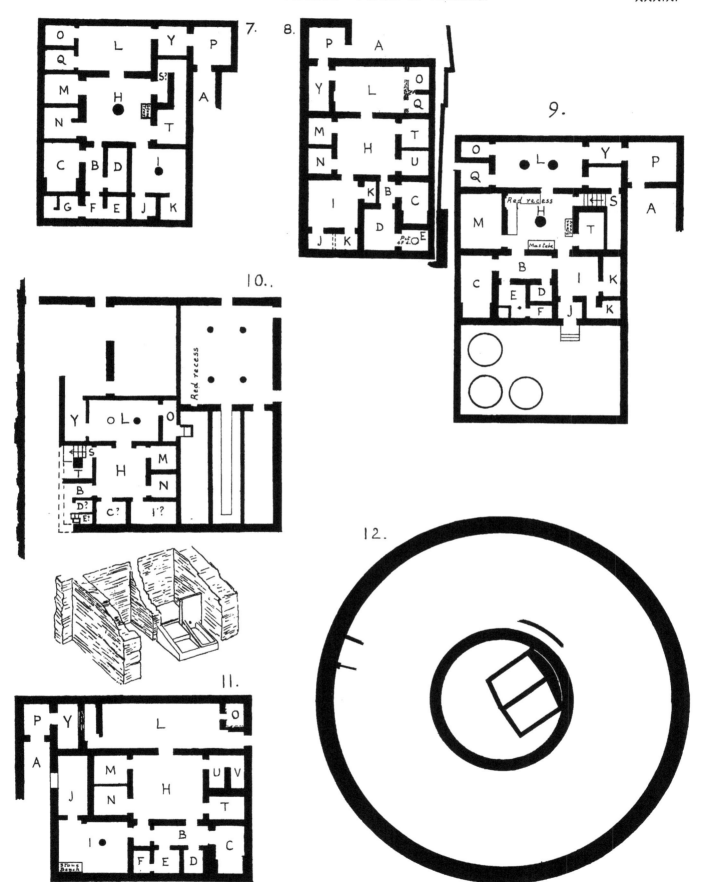

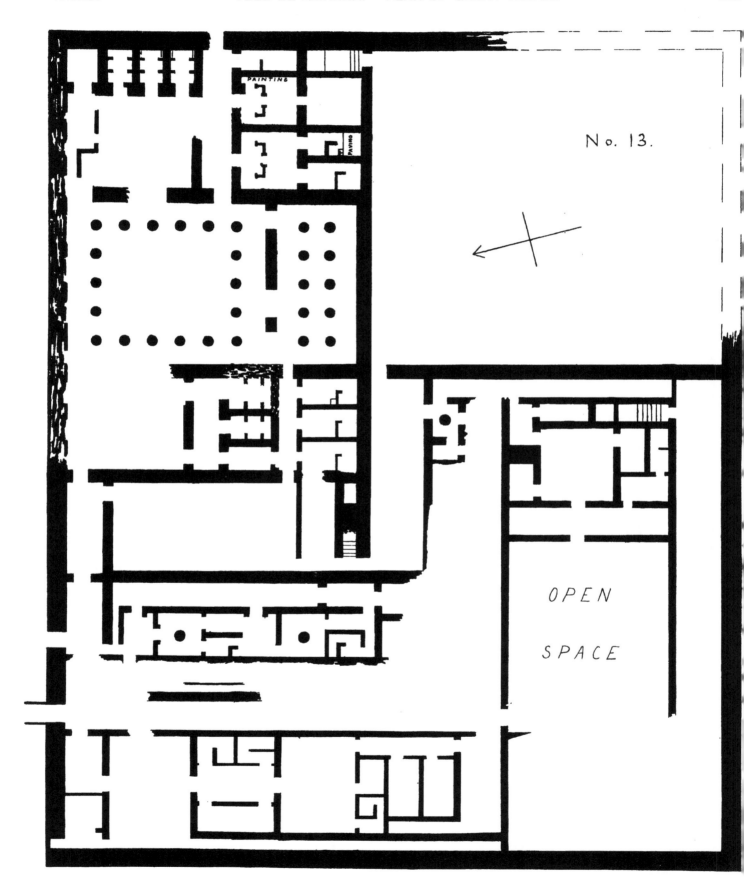

PAINTING

PAINTING

No. 13.

OPEN

SPACE

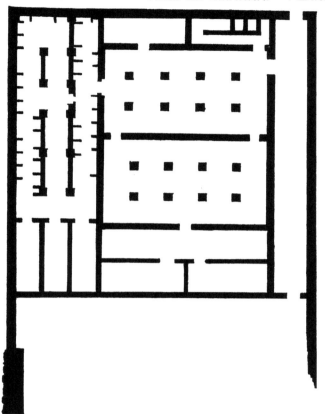

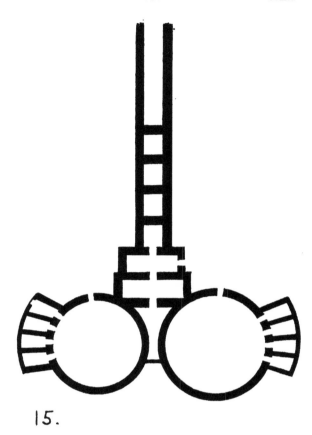

15.

14.

16.

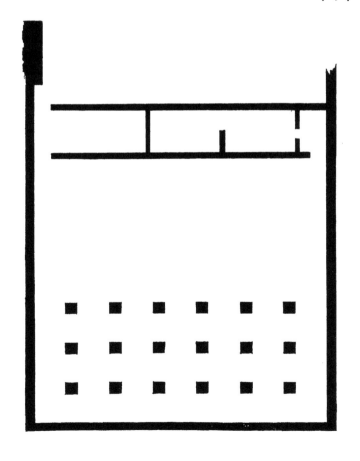

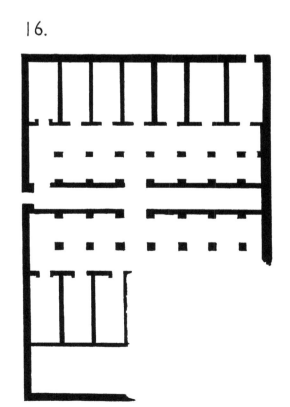

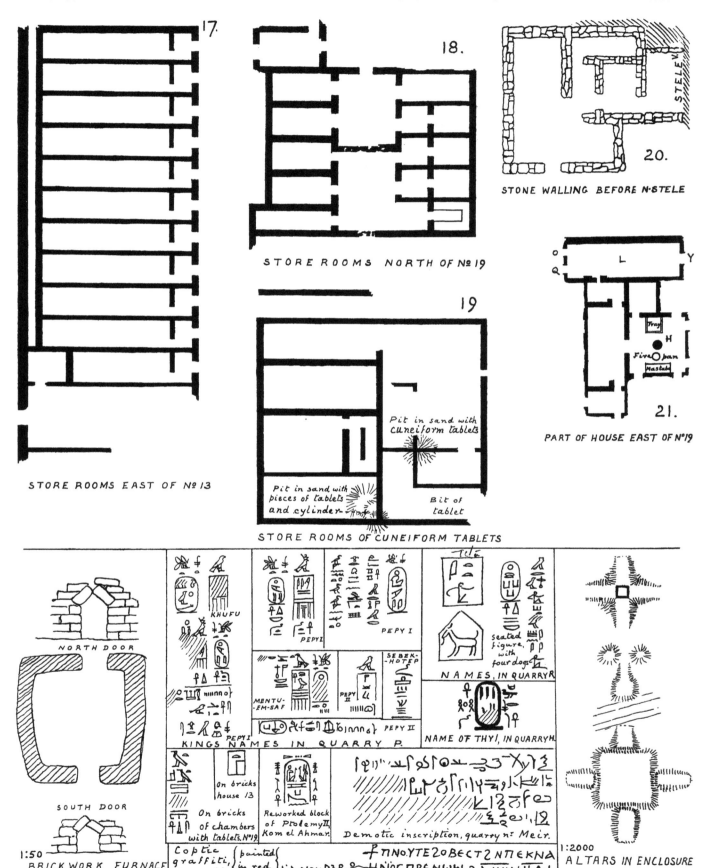

17.

18.

20.

STONE WALLING BEFORE N·STELE

STORE ROOMS NORTH OF Nº 19

19.

Pit in sand with cuneiform tablets

21.

PART OF HOUSE EAST OF Nº 19

STORE ROOMS EAST OF Nº 13

Pit in sand with pieces of tablets and cylinder

Bit of tablet

STORE ROOMS OF CUNEIFORM TABLETS

NORTH DOOR

KHUFU

PEPY I

PEPY I

NAMES, IN QUARRY R

PEPY I

MENTU-EM-SAF

SEBEK-HOTEP

PEPY II

PEPY II

NAME OF THYI, IN QUARRY H.

KINGS NAMES IN QUARRY P.

SOUTH DOOR

On bricks house 13

On bricks of chambers with tablets. Nº 19

Reworked block of Ptolemy II Kom el Ahmar.

Demotic inscription, quarry nr Meir.

1:50

BRICKWORK FURNACE IN GLAZING FACTORY.

Coptic graffiti, Bawit.

painted in red

charcoal writing on plaster

+ ΠΝΟΥΤΕ2ΟΒΕСΤ2ΝΠΙΕΚΝΑ
+ΑΝΟΚΒ̄Ρ̄οˤ ΗΝΟСΠΡΕΝΝΨΣ2ΑΜΗΝϤΘ+
+ΠΝΟΥΤΕ2ϤΙ4ΖΙΝΔ

1:2000

ALTARS IN ENCLOSURE BEFORE NORTH TOMBS.

For EU product safety concerns, contact us at Calle de José Abascal, 56–1°,
28003 Madrid, Spain or eugpsr@cambridge.org.

www.ingramcontent.com/pod-product-compliance
Ingram Content Group UK Ltd.
Pitfield, Milton Keynes, MK11 3LW, UK
UKHW051030150625
459647UK00023B/2871